Every human bein[g] is an exploration o[f] invitation to look th[rough] and back at our own. *Such self-reflection is essential* to transformation, and there is no place safer than inside the holy ground of another person's story.
William Paul Young, author of *The Shack*

If you have a dream inside you and want to know how to make your dream come true, you must read this book! Dream Chasers *is full of spiritual insights and practical life lessons from those who have navigated through setbacks, disappointments, and hardships while holding on to their dreams. You will get hungry to pick up your dream again and know how to pursue greatness!*
Les Brown, motivational speaker and author of *Live Your Dreams*

This is an encouraging book with testimonies of several of us, but all of you who are reading this book have a dream, and it started with a dream from the heart of God. As you chase the dream in your life and overcome the challenges and obstacles on your way, you will be fulfilled, and you will see God working through you.
Loren Cunningham, founder of Youth With A Mission (YWAM) and author of *Is it Really You, God?*

Dream Chasers *is a book that encourages the reader to pursue the fullness of their calling and destiny. This is a book about getting up when life knocks you down. It is about taking risks and seeing the glory of God's kingdom come in all its fullness. It is about how love changes everything. It is a book that must be read!*
Canon Andrew White, Vicar Emeritus of Baghdad, author of *Faith Under Fire* and *The*

Vicar of Baghdad

Dream Chasers *is a great project that gets to
the heart of the challenge of the Christian life:
navigating through seasons of pain and contradiction
by trusting God, who is always good. You can't help
but be inspired as you read the stories of the trials and
victories of some of my personal heroes. I'm sure you
will find hope and courage to follow through on your
own journey as you pursue your destiny and fulfil
your God-given dreams.*

**Bill Johnson, senior pastor at Bethel Church,
and author of *When Heaven Invades Earth* and
*God Is Good***

*This book is encouraging, thought-provoking,
inspiring, and very well written. It will impact
everyone who reads it! We all have dreams; the
challenge is finding how to live them out. We can
learn from the stories told in this book of how to
work with the Lord in fulfilling the dreams he's put
on our hearts for the world in which we live.*

**Sally McClung, missionary and co-founder of
All Nations, South Africa**

DREAM CHASERS

The Journey of Nine Ordinary People
Who Became Extraordinary

Uta Schmidt

LION

Published by
Lion Hudson Limited
Wilkinson House, Jordan Hill Business Park
Banbury Road, Oxford OX2 8DR, England
www.lionhudson.com

ISBN 9780745980652
e-ISBN 9780745980669

First edition 2018

Acknowledgments
Unless otherwise stated, Scripture quotations are taken from the New King James Version (NKJV). Copyright © 1982 by Thomas Nelson, Inc. Used by permission. All rights reserved.

Also cited:

The Holy Bible, New Living Translation (NLT), copyright © 1996, 2004, 2007 by Tyndale House Foundation. Used by permission of Tyndale House Publishers, Inc., Carol Stream, Illinois 60188. All rights reserved.

The New Revised Standard Version Bible: Anglicised Edition (NRSVA), copyright © 1989, 1995 the Division of Christian Education of the National Council of the Churches of Christ in the United States of America. Used by permission. All rights reserved.

The New American Standard Bible® (NASB), Copyright © 1960, 1962, 1963, 1968, 1971, 1972, 1973, 1975, 1977, 1995 by The Lockman Foundation. Used by permission.

The Holy Bible, New International Version. Anglicised (NIV UK). Copyright © 1979, 1984, 2011 Biblica, formerly International Bible Society. Used by permission of Hodder & Stoughton Ltd, an Hachette UK company. All rights reserved. "NIV" is a registered trademark of Biblica. UK trademark number 1448790.

A catalogue record for this book is available from the British Library

Printed and bound in the UK, October 2018, LH26

Cover design by Uta Schmidt, Arjun Neupane, Bart den Hartog, and Clair Lansley

Cover images: © iulias, © Attitude (Shutterstock); © Darrin Giddens (bsnscb.com)

Contents

Foreword

by Canon Andrew White
Vicar Emeritus of Baghdad

I am often asked to write forewords for books. I often read books which really would have been of great use in my former profession of putting people to sleep (I was an anaesthetist)... But this book is different! It is different because it is about people who do not take care, but rather take risks for the kingdom of God!

This book looks at some of the giants of the faith. It is the intimate story of those who have realized in life that the problem to walking in our destiny is not stumbling or falling; rather, the problem is not getting up. It includes the stories of Desmond Tutu (Archbishop Emeritus of Cape Town), William Paul Young (author of *The Shack*), Les Brown (inspirational speaker), Bill Johnson (pastor of Bethel Church, Redding), Loren Cunningham (founder of Youth With A Mission), Rolland and Heidi Baker (Iris Ministries, Mozambique) and Dr Sandra Kennedy (Whole Life Ministries).

All of these people have experienced setbacks and have fallen in their journey of life, but they have also gotten up again. And because these people did, they have made a difference not just in their own community, but also across the world. This is a book we must all read, learn from, and absorb.

Dream Chasers is a book that indeed allows and encourages the reader to get up and pursue the fullness of their calling and destiny. It challenges the reader to not be complacent, but to see what's possible and to join in the battle to truly establish God's kingdom in its majesty and glory. This is a book about getting up when life knocks you down. It is about taking risks and seeing the glory of the kingdom come in all its fullness. It is about how love changes everything. It is a book that must be read.

Introduction

What stands between you and your dream?

A new perspective on obstacles

Hope deferred makes the heart sick, but a dream
fulfilled is a tree of life.
Proverbs 13:12 (NLT)

Have you ever known the pain and disappointment of a
shattered dream, a hope deferred, a vision put on hold, or
a desire placed on the back burner? Maybe you started out with
a dream in your heart, but it has been buried beneath the rubble
of life's challenges. Or you set out with a great vision or a call
for ministry – and then life happened. And it did not happen
the way you expected. Maybe your marriage didn't work out,
maybe you got stuck in a career you never really anticipated,
maybe you lost a loved one, or maybe your trust was broken
by people you thought were reliable. Whatever it was, life took
some unexpected turns and threw you off course.

I don't know which of the above situations you most relate
to. But there is one thing I know about you: you are a dream
chaser. I know this because you have picked up this book. You
have a deep yearning for your dream to come true, for your
destiny to be fulfilled. You know that God has more for you
than you are experiencing right now. Deep inside, the hope that
was deferred is whispering and knocking on the door of your
heart, reminding you that God is the dream giver and that it is
time to dare to dream again.

Here is something else I know about you: you have encountered obstacles as you've chased your dream. Maybe you have struggled to overcome the limitations of your thinking or insecurities. Or you just can't break through your fears, and they have been holding you back. Maybe you are dealing with the shattered pieces of a broken past that keep you in bondage and don't allow you to walk in the freedom you were hoping to find. Maybe you have been battling illness, or you have experienced emotional wounds, betrayal, or disappointment. Or maybe your heart is just sick because your hope has been deferred. And you wonder if these obstacles will keep you from reaching your dream.

You've probably also picked up this book because you want to know how other dream chasers have pursued their dreams. Maybe the thought has crossed your mind – like it did mine – that the grass must be greener on the other side of the fence. Perhaps you believe that successful dream chasers must have it easier than you do, and can't possibly have faced obstacles like those you've encountered. Or you might just assume that they succeeded because they had a calling that you don't have – a special calling that came with special favour from God. Let me tell you: nothing is further from the truth than that.

Why this book?

So many of us struggle or see contradictions between our perceived purpose and our circumstances. And yet most of us feel alone when this happens. As a Christian life coach, I have taught leadership and personal development courses in both Christian and secular environments for years. And I have observed that the vast majority of books, manuals, and training courses on success provide little to no guidance on dealing with setbacks and navigating challenging seasons. And yet I believe it is exactly this experience of navigating setbacks that forms a successful dream chaser.

Personally, I have experienced more than just one season of contradiction in my life. But one of the most defining ones came for me in 2011, when my life was hit by a "perfect storm" of hardships. The experience totally threw me off course, and I found myself asking some tough questions about life, my calling from God, and what role I played in all of it. I concluded that I must have simply missed God's will, or else these contradictions wouldn't be happening to me – until I came across a study on destiny conducted by Dr Robert Clinton, a professor at Fuller Theological Seminary, which taught me otherwise.

In his empirical research, Dr Clinton collected data from individual case studies for more than thirty years, and he found that 80 per cent of his research subjects felt they had not fulfilled their ultimate life call, while only 20 per cent believed that they had. When he analyzed the difference between the two groups, he concluded that the primary reason why the 80 per cent did not walk out their full destiny was that they did not understand the maturing process necessary to get there. Specifically, they did not know how to deal with the experiences of life that stood in contradiction to their dream. Experiences such as tragedy, loss, disappointment, setbacks, or resistance – in short, suffering. They became mired in the contradictions. As did I.

The findings from Clinton's research and his consequent Leadership Emergence Theory can be found in his book *The Making of a Leader*. Reading that book started me on another quest. If it is true that every individual God uses to impact this world with his purposes must undergo a refining process, and that that process consists of contradictory experiences, then I wanted to find out what contradictions some of my heroes had gone through. I also wanted to know what had actually helped them navigate through their dark seasons of life. I wanted to find out what sets successful dream chasers apart from those who have a vision but ultimately fail to achieve it.

Through exclusive interviews with nine extraordinary leaders, I have discovered that those who succeed in chasing the dream God has given them do not avoid life's contradictions and hardships. They are not immune to the pain of them. They endure suffering and experience crises of faith, often in greater supply than the average person does. But ultimately they find a way through them.

And we can do the same on the way to our God-given dreams.

In this book, I share the stories of nine high-profile leaders who have fought great battles in private, before or even while their victories were paraded in public. Those leaders are: Desmond Tutu, Nobel Peace Prize laureate and Archbishop Emeritus of Cape Town; world-renowned inspirational speaker Les Brown; William Paul Young, author of the worldwide bestselling novel *The Shack*; peace negotiator in the Middle East Canon Andrew White, also known as the Vicar of Baghdad; Bill Johnson, senior pastor of Bethel Church in Redding, California; Loren Cunningham, founder of the worldwide mission movement Youth With A Mission (YWAM); Rolland and Heidi Baker, missionaries and founders of Iris Ministries, Mozambique; and author and pastor Dr Sandra Kennedy.

Why these dream chasers?

Why did I choose these leaders? In some cases, an opportunity for an interview simply arose as I pursued this project. Other interviews I adamantly sought until I succeeded. Of course, I approached more leaders than those represented in this book, but not everyone was available for an interview at the time. My criteria for selecting the leaders were these: first, they had to have lived long enough to really have something to say, and the preferred age was fifty-five or older. Next, they needed to have a proven track record of integrity. In addition, they needed to have fulfilled a considerable part of their dream. Finally,

I approached leaders whom I considered to be honest and transparent enough to share their struggles and weaknesses, not just their glories and breakthrough experiences.

One thing I did not want to do was interview leaders from only one Christian stream or denomination. Instead, I wanted to obtain the perspectives of a variety of leaders from different walks of life. I desired to have a broader view on this topic to get out of the box of a specific theological framework.

My intention is not to promote a specific theological view, organization, or denomination. Nor do I want to focus on where we differ. Instead, I wish to uncover the obstacles, the challenges, and the development processes of these specific individuals, and to examine what all humans experience: pain.

All of that being said, I do have a personal connection with each of the leaders I interviewed. They all generously shared with me from their lifetime of experience, which provided a wealth of information worth more than gold.

I started by interviewing Loren Cunningham, founder of Youth With A Mission (YWAM), because his story had a great impact on my life in my early twenties when I read his book, *Is That Really You, God?* It led me to actually participate in Youth With A Mission (YWAM) from 1993 to 1995, near Cape Town, South Africa. To me, Loren Cunningham is a kind of Moses figure. He has tremendous influence but he exhibits real humility. He also has an incredibly close relationship with God, and a wealth of wisdom, gained from his more than eighty years of life experience.

During my time in South Africa with YWAM, I witnessed the first democratic election in the nation and the transfer of power from the Afrikaans apartheid government to the first black ANC government, with Nelson Mandela as president. I've always been fascinated with Africa, and South Africa's history and experience gripped my heart. Being able to witness this historic transition of power had a lasting impact on my life.

My big dream was to interview Nelson Mandela, but I took too long to overcome my limited way of thinking and step into my dream. By the time I began my interviews, Mandela's health had already taken a bad turn, and he died shortly thereafter. However, I held on to the motto "dream big", and put my second greatest hero, Desmond Tutu, on the list instead. For me, this was a faith project, as I saw no possibility in the natural to make this happen. But I just wanted to see if God could do it, or rather if he *would* do it for me. And he did. And that story alone is worth another book.

I approached Les Brown for an interview during one of my first intensive speakers' training courses with him. Les Brown has had a significant impact on my life, by pulling me into my destiny, breaking through my fears and limited way of thinking, and helping me to develop a healthy mindset. When he speaks the words "You've got greatness in you!" they impact the heart of the listener and open the door for a transformation. And they started transforming me. He saw something in me that I couldn't see and instilled the faith into me that it was possible to step into my dream. He believed in me and in this project, and this has encouraged me to take some bold steps in pursuing more of my dream and calling. I'm ever so grateful for him!

With Dr Sandra Kennedy, an opportunity for an interview presented itself when I travelled to Augusta, Georgia, in 2015. An unmarried female preacher coming from a Southern Baptist background, she established a multiracial church in the 1970s. Even though the experiences of her vision and calling were very unique, most of us can identify with the struggles she has had to overcome on the way to pursuing her dream. Moreover, she had something to share about the challenges she encountered as an unmarried female leader, which I consider very important to address in the Christian community.

Other interviews I pursued adamantly for up to two years, such as the interview with the author of *The Shack*, William

Paul Young. I went to great lengths to hear his personal history from him because I knew his story of emotional healing would be an extremely significant chapter in this book. I believe there is still a great lack of understanding of what this process of inner healing from traumatic events entails, particularly within the Christian community.

Bill Johnson is a pillar of wisdom, and the experience of worship at his church, Bethel, invigorates my soul and draws me deeper into God's presence. I'm grateful for the teaching I've received through Bethel, and Bill's wisdom on the tough issues of life has brought healing to my heart. He is so down to earth and real, and the interview with him impacted me deeply. Since then I've had experiences that have reminded me of what Bill shared with me, and I've put it into practice in my own life. I'm deeply grateful for his time and his support in this project.

Rolland and Heidi Baker are true heroes of faith. In 2008 and 2009 I spent some time with Iris Ministries in Mozambique and attended their Mission Training School. At that time, Rolland's life was hanging by a thread. When I began this project, I was confident that if I wanted to know more about dealing with obstacles and contradictions, Rolland and Heidi would have plenty to share.

I first heard about their ministry in 2007, and Heidi's example of radical love for Jesus and the poorest of the poor made a deep impression on me. I was immediately convicted of my own lack of passion. Spending time in Mozambique showed me the kind of relationship with God that was possible for a human being, and this created a deep hunger in me to pursue more of him. After attending their mission school, my life was transformed. On looking back, I can still see how much of Heidi's example to love well has remained with me.

I approached Canon Andrew White because I wanted to present more than just a Western point of view on the topic of pursuing your dream. Although all the leaders I interviewed are genuine and do not embrace a modern prosperity gospel, I felt it necessary to hear from a representative of the persecuted church in the Middle East. I specifically wanted to know how the people there deal with their shattered dreams. Andrew White is British, but he lived in Baghdad for nearly fifteen years, and he knows intimately the suffering of the persecuted church in Iraq. He is also an expert on the conflicts in the Middle East, and what he has to share will convict and at the same time encourage you.

My interviews usually lasted one to two hours, with the exception of my time with Desmond Tutu. Owing to protocol and his fragile health, I had limited time with him. In order to present a comprehensive picture of his struggle, I have carried out extensive research and consulted several other sources to fill in the gaps and present a more in-depth portrayal. All of those sources are clearly listed in the footnotes, and Archbishop Tutu has personally reviewed and approved the representation of his story in Chapter Nine, "Wounded Healers".

In the chapters about the other leaders, I have done the same and added important details based on biographies and other books. This was often necessary to fully describe the person and the context of the conflict and contradiction they experienced. I have woven the interviews into the main storyline and indicated where I refer to other sources. All chapters have been reviewed, modified where necessary, and approved by each of the interviewees themselves to ensure the accuracy of the content and the portrayal of their stories.

This book fills a hole in the Christian leadership market by unearthing what we can learn from the great role models of our time about overcoming obstacles and emerging victorious. As you read this book, you will learn what it really means to live your life to the fullest, gain insight into the realities of the journey God takes us through, learn how to deal with shattered dreams, and grow in determination to follow your God-given dreams straight through the fire of transformation.

Dr Larry Crabb put it this way: "Shattered dreams are never random. They are always a piece in a larger puzzle, a chapter in a larger story." He explains, "The Holy Spirit uses the pain of shattered dreams to help us discover our desire for God, to help us begin dreaming the highest dream. They are ordained opportunities for the Spirit to awaken, then to satisfy our highest dream."[1] This is what you will discover in the inspiring stories shared throughout this book. I am convinced that you will find hope and a new perspective on your own journey.

Chapter One
Prisoners of Destiny

A training for reigning

Nelson Mandela, Moses, Joseph

> Life only makes sense backward, but we have to live
> it forward.
>
> *Dag Hammersjørd*

His father gave him the name Rolihlahla, which means "troublemaker". For the first part of his adult life, this name would turn out to be rather prophetic. In fact, he stirred up strife and trouble throughout a whole nation to fight injustice. His Methodist teacher gave him the English name Nelson, which means "son of a champion". In the latter part of his life, he would be known to the whole world as one of the greatest peacemakers of our time, and as a champion who chose reconciliation above justice and thus saved a whole nation from genocide: Nelson Rolihlahla Mandela.

Something happened between the first part and the latter part of his life, between owning the reputation of "troublemaker" and becoming a peacemaker: a transformation process that took twenty-seven years.

This chapter explores the transformation process in the life of Nelson Mandela, as well as the lives of the two biblical leaders Moses and Joseph. All three examples show a similar pattern of development orchestrated by God to prepare them for the task they were ultimately called to fulfil. The biblical accounts offer valuable insights into the process of chasing a dream, and the more recent example of Nelson Mandela shows that God's ways of shaping a leader and preparing him for his destiny have not changed. So let's dig a little deeper into their *story*, which occurred before they made *history*.

From troublemaker to peacemaker

Nelson was born a Xhosa prince within the Thembu royal family. Although he was not eligible for succession to the Xhosa throne, members of his clan inherited the position of royal counsellors, and, as such, a clear path was laid out for Nelson, with a promising future.

Nelson spent his childhood as a shepherd and herds boy. Both of his parents were illiterate, but his mother was a devout Christian and sent him to a local Methodist school when he was seven years old so that he could learn to read and write.

When Nelson was nine, his father died, and Nelson was adopted by the Xhosa king. His father had done a great favour for the king, and now the Xhosa chief returned the favour by taking on the education of his advisor's son. Nelson grew up in the royal household, with all the privileges of comfort and education that a royal tribal household could offer. His upbringing was designed to prepare him to step into his father's shoes and become a royal counsellor to his adoptive brother Justice, the future king of the Xhosa people.

But his life would take a different turn from the path his guardian had laid out for him. One day, at the age of twenty-two, after the king had announced to Nelson and Justice that he had arranged marriages for them, Nelson decided to run away, to break with tradition and pursue a different course. He would study law in Johannesburg and later marry for love.

After the initial excitement of his new life working as a clerk in a Johannesburg law firm had faded, Nelson began to wake up to a new reality. For the first time, he was outside the tribal territory of the royal Xhosa household and confronted with the abject oppression of his fellow African people throughout the land. Mandela describes the fierce discrimination blacks faced in his book, *Long Walk To Freedom*:

> For blacks it was a crime to walk through a whites only door, a crime to ride a whites only bus, a crime to use a whites only drinking fountain, a crime to not have a pass book and a crime to have a wrong signature in the pass book. It was a crime to be unemployed and a crime to be employed in the wrong place, a crime to live in certain places and a crime to have no place to live.[1]

In the early stages of his law career he resisted getting involved in politics, specifically with the Communist Party, since he was opposed to their atheistic views. But as he was confronted with the daily injustices against his people as a lawyer who was attempting to defend their rights, he became more politicized and eventually took up the national struggle for his fellow Africans with the African National Congress (ANC).

Initially it was the ANC's conviction that non-violent resistance was the path to bringing about change in the political situation. This approach, however, had little to no effect. The new government was unrelenting, even going so far as to expand racial segregation with the new apartheid legislation of the National Party in 1948. As the oppression increased, Mandela became desperate and called for a revolution and militant resistance.

Hunted by the government, he had to go underground. While in exile, he recruited support from neighbouring African nations for his guerrilla warfare plans, but upon returning to South Africa to implement the first act of sabotage in October

1953, Mandela was betrayed and captured. Together with several other ANC leaders, he was charged and convicted of high treason, which, according to the law, would demand the death sentence. On the day of sentencing, the atmosphere was charged, and everyone expected the inevitable as the judge prepared to announce the verdict. But by a miracle – and as a result of international pressure – the Supreme Court refrained from capital punishment and instead sentenced Mandela and his fellow accused to life in prison.

"Amandla!" Mandela shouted to the crowd in the court as he was led away and disappeared from the stage of political activism. This was the Zulu and Xhosa word for "power". His fellow prisoners shouted, *"Awethu!"* which means "to us". The shouts became a symbolic representation of the struggle against apartheid and oppression in South Africa, demanding that political power be given to the people. They emphasized that the struggle against the oppressive regime would not end.

Mandela would end up spending twenty-seven years in prison. During that time he came to realize that violence was not the solution. He would emerge from prison with an agenda other than reciprocal aggression to free his people from oppression: he emerged with an agenda of forgiveness and reconciliation toward the oppressors. His negotiations for a peaceful resolution saved a whole nation from a genocide of a magnitude that, according to experts, was far greater than that of the Rwandan genocide of 1994. Through his leadership, Nelson Mandela reconciled blacks and whites, coloureds and Indians, oppressor and oppressed.

The rest is history.

Prince of Egypt

About 5,000 years earlier, in northern Africa, a boy was born to a people who had hopes and dreams of one day being delivered from their oppressors and living in dignity and freedom in a land they could call their own. His parents believed so fervently in a better future for him that they risked their own lives to protect his life from the king's attempt to kill him.

When they chose non-violent resistance to save him and were hiding his existence from the authorities, they had no way of knowing that their offspring was destined to save their entire nation from the iron fist of tyranny.

Moshe Ben Amram – also known as Moses – was born a beautiful boy to the Levi clan of the Hebrew people enslaved in Egypt, at a time when his people were increasing in numbers and the Egyptian king was worried that they might overpower them or join forces with Egypt's enemies. Moses' mother, a devout believer in God, hid him when the pharaoh ordered that all newborn Hebrew boys be killed. Pharaoh had issued this decree in response to a rumoured prophecy of a messianic deliverer who was soon to arise among the Hebrew slaves. Moses' mother and sister placed him in a basket in the River Nile, where Pharaoh's daughter, Queen Bithiah, found him. When she saw the baby, she adopted him as her own.

From hero to zero

We don't know if this is the name his parents gave him, but Exodus 2 says that Pharaoh's daughter called him Moshe (Moses), which means "drawn out of the water". As an adopted member of the Egyptian royal family, Moshe enjoyed all the privileges of comfort and education that a royal household could offer. And yet, one day, he had to run away. He saw the cruelty of the oppression of his people, and witnessed it in silence for a long time. But one day his response was different: he took action. When a merciless guard severely mistreated one of his Hebrew brothers, Moshe's temper got the better of him and he answered relentless violence with violent resistance. But the moment he raised his hand against the Egyptian slave master and killed him, Moshe became a wanted fugitive.

Moshe went underground and fled across the Red Sea to Midian – a territory that stretches from modern-day southern Jordan to western Saudi Arabia, southern Israel and the Egyptian Sinai peninsula. There he served his own sentence of solitary confinement, far from the privileges and prestige of the royal household, and from his Egyptian and Hebrew family and friends. This sentence lasted forty years, in a parched desert, herding sheep. It was there that Moshe encountered God in the burning bush, and finally returned to Egypt to secure the release of his people from slavery.

The rest is history.

The coat of many colours

About 400 years earlier than Moses, a boy was born to a prince called Yisrael, also known as Jacob. Joseph was then the youngest of Jacob's eleven sons and considered a miracle child, since his mother Rachel, Jacob's first love, had been barren for many years. While his half-brothers had to herd the flocks, Joseph enjoyed all the privileges and education Jacob's household could offer.

This set the stage for the dramatic plot that was about to unfold. The brothers, already jealous of Joseph because of Jacob's favouritism, were even more incensed when Joseph received a beautiful coat of many colours from their father. They saw this as an indication that Joseph would take over as clan leader upon Jacob's death, despite being the youngest.

The plot thickened when Joseph told his brothers of two dreams he'd had, in which they all bowed down to him (Genesis 37:5–11). Announcing to his brothers that they would serve him was not the smartest move – as he would soon find out. The narrative tells that his brothers began to plot against him when he was a teenager, about seventeen years old. They were ready to kill him, but thanks to an intricate subplot penned by the superior hand of God, they decided instead to sell him as a slave to a company of Ishmaelite merchants.

Joseph was taken away from home to a foreign land, exiled, sold as a slave to an Egyptian master, thrown into prison for a crime he did not commit, betrayed, and forgotten for several years, spending his existence in a dungeon with other Egyptian criminals. But one day the plot took an unexpected turn. About two decades after being sold into slavery in Egypt, Joseph was named vice-pharaoh in the land of his affliction. Soon afterward, his brothers, plagued by a great famine, went down to Egypt to buy grain to save their families from starvation. They bowed down before the Egyptian ruler, unaware that he was their brother. And in spite of their betrayal, Joseph saved them, along with their families, and established them in a safe land.

The rest is history.

The dream process

What do these three history makers have in common? Hidden within each account of someone who made history is a personal story: one of hardship, loss, disappointment, contradiction, and injustice. On the way to their destiny, all three had to go through a refining process, where they had to face and overcome deep life issues. This process developed their character and prepared them so that they could fulfil their future destiny.

I have always been fascinated by the biblical account of Joseph and revelled in the happy ending. But here is the difference between Joseph and us: we know how the story ends, but Joseph didn't. We know his story backward, but he had to live it forward.

This is also the case with our own lives when we face contradictions, disappointments, betrayals, difficulties, and setbacks. Often, we are so deep in a pit that we don't know whether we will ever get out again. Nelson Mandela didn't know if he would ever get out of prison and be able to hold his wife and children again. Moses didn't know if he would ever set foot in Egypt and see his family again. Joseph didn't know if he would ever get out of prison and see his father again.

The challenge is that life only makes sense looking backward, but when we are in the thick of it, we have to live it forward. Emotions are raw, wounds infected, and disappointments real. Our minds are faced with thoughts we didn't even know we were capable of conceiving. This is the place where we are faced with the enemies on the inside that seek to destroy our soul. The battle is fierce, and we often get bruised or beaten up. But it is exactly here where we learn to win the internal battle, so that later we will be able to stand strong and not be destroyed by any enemy from the outside. An African proverb puts it this way: "If there is no enemy from within, the enemy from without can do you no harm."

The account of Joseph's story doesn't give away any details about the inward struggle he was going through as he was facing betrayal, disappointments, and injustice. But one thing is clear: it was a painful process. It prepared him for the ultimate assignment he was called to, which required refined character and faith. Later in the Bible, Joseph's situation is described in this way: "His feet were hurt with fetters, his neck was put in a collar of iron; until what he had said came to pass, the word of the Lord kept testing him" (Psalm 105:18–19, NRSVA). The Hebrew word translated into English as "testing" means "purging gold or silver by fire in order to separate it from the impurities", and its metaphorical use refers to testing, proving, trying, and examining someone's motives.[2] Joseph was tested on multiple levels during his life to prepare him for the fulfilment of his dream. And the greater the dream, the more thorough the testing and preparation.

The internal battle

We don't know what the most difficult test for Joseph was, but, reading between the lines, it appears very likely that it was the battle from within – not the slavery or imprisonment from without. The toughest test for Joseph was betrayal, and that hits deeper and far closer to the heart than any external oppression. The betrayal of his brothers – his own flesh and blood – must have pierced him so deeply that twenty years later when his brothers bowed down before him, Joseph was still affected by it. He immediately ran away and wept. I doubt his weeping was prompted by feelings of warmth and joy at the prospect of a reunion with his brothers. He tested them at first, and I believe that, as he was testing them, he himself had to conquer some residue of pain and conflicting emotions, until he came to the conclusion, "You meant evil against me, but God meant it for good" (Genesis 50:20). This statement marked the conclusion of a process for a man who had wrestled with God, his destiny, and his heart – but he overcame by faith and by holding the course, until the promise came to pass.

When Nelson Mandela started to engage in the freedom struggle, he was aware of the possibility of imprisonment and the hardships that would bring. But being separated from his wife and unable to see his children grow up was far more difficult than he had expected. In his book, he describes the moment when he caught a last glimpse of his wife after being sentenced to life in prison: "It is one thing to be told of possible hardships ahead of time. It is an entirely different one to actually have to confront them."[3]

As with Joseph, it was not the insults, the beatings, the humiliations by the guards, or the confinement to a cell that affected Mandela most deeply. The issues that injured his heart on a more personal level were far more difficult to conquer. One day a guard came to his cell at an unexpected hour and dropped a piece of paper through the bars. "Mandela, there is a message for you!" he mechanically recited. It was a telegram. Mandela opened it, expecting to read that perhaps his mother had taken a bad turn or passed away. Instead, to his great consternation, he read that his firstborn son Tembe had died in a car accident. Stricken by grief, Mandela asked the prison director for permission to arrange and attend his son's funeral – under the surveillance of guards – explaining that it was his responsibility as a father to do so. But the warden showed no sympathy and coldly denied his request. After that conversation, Mandela returned to his cell and did not speak a word for two entire days. He just sat there in silence, struggling to process the pain and loss.

What was the toughest issue for Moses? It was probably a sense of failure, the feeling that he had blown it. Moses must have known about the expectation of a deliverer among the Hebrew slaves, for it is likely that he was still in contact with his family while he was growing up in the Egyptian palace. Moses must have had a sense of destiny when he considered his miraculous rescue and upbringing in the Egyptian palace. But his premature attempt to help his people had failed, and now he was exiled. When God appeared to him in the burning bush and told him to go back to Egypt to demand the release of his people, Moses argued that he wasn't the right person for that job. "I can't do it; I can't speak! Let someone else do it!" was his response (Exodus 3:11; 4:10, 13). Overcoming the sense of failure and believing that God could still use him was one of his greatest tests.

Prisoners of destiny

Joseph had to deal with real-life issues, with raw emotions, and with extreme contradictions. Most of the time he must have felt as far away from the fulfilment of his juvenile leadership dream as one can imagine: being a slave in a foreign land, and later not only a slave but an accused criminal as well. That's about as low as you can get. Any hope that his dream would ever materialize in his life must have faded into nothingness.

This is true for all three leaders. They all had a dream in their hearts; more specifically, a dream that was far beyond their reach, and it seemed impossible that it would become a reality. They all went through a process whereby their dream was shattered, whereby the possibility of the fulfilment of their heart's desire seemed a delusion, nothing more than a vain notion. However, in this valley of the shadow of death they developed strength of character, humility, and perseverance. They conquered their enemies from within, so that ultimately they could not be conquered by any enemy from without.

"Perhaps it requires such depth of oppression to create such heights of character," Nelson Mandela writes, referring to an unexpected side effect of his and his people's experience. It had produced men of extraordinary courage, wisdom, and generosity who fought alongside him. He concludes his detailed account of his freedom struggle with this statement: "My country is rich in the minerals and gems that lie beneath this soil, but I have always known that its greatest wealth is its people – finer and truer than the purest diamonds."[4]

Many dream chasers throughout history have experienced shipwreck on their journey in pursuit of their dream. Both the outside circumstances and the battles within threatened to conquer them. Unable to see the turnaround that was to come, they struggled with discouragement and despair. Because we can see the end of the story, we can see their struggles as part of a preparatory process. This perspective doesn't make our own refining process any easier, but it can help us navigate through the seasons of contradiction so that we hold the course and don't give up on the vision, calling, and dream in our hearts.

The fulfilment of our dreams is intended to serve not only our own good, but also a greater good, whose impact we cannot yet foresee. This is what 1 Corinthians 2:9 means when it says, "No eye has seen, no ear has heard, and no mind has imagined what God has prepared for those who love him" (NLT). We don't see the full picture when living life forward and going through the preparatory process, but when we hold the course, we will look backward and see the great design.

In the end, the fulfilment of Joseph's dream had everything to do with timing. If he had been released from prison through the cupbearer's help before the "right" time, it is very likely he would have left Egypt and returned to his father. In doing that, he would have missed his ultimate assignment and the manifestation of his dream. So, even as he remained unfairly imprisoned, Joseph wasn't a prisoner of his circumstances – he was a *prisoner of his destiny*. He would be released into the right position at the right time for a greater good. The same is true for your journey of dream fulfilment. In the face of seeming contradictions, it's crucial to hold the course. You are *not* a prisoner of circumstances. You are a prisoner of destiny!

Scripture tells us to "not think it strange concerning the fiery trial which is to try you, as though some strange thing happened unto you" (1 Peter 4:12). Very often, though, we do think it "strange" when we face difficulties and setbacks, when life takes a different turn from the one we expected. We tend to assume that the road to our destiny is laid out smoothly, and that blessing and favour will pave the way before us. One reason for this is that Western culture and Western churches focus on the victory and success parts of people's stories. We simply do not hear about the battle that preceded the victory. That's unfortunate, because when we understand that the refining process is experienced by everyone, we're more capable of seeing our own process all the way through, until the fulfilment of the promise materializes.

I believe one reason why the biblical account does not give us exact details of Moses' or Joseph's internal struggles is that every person's process is different. If the Bible gave us more details, someone would probably have written a "Three-step action plan to success", or a "How to overcome your crisis" plan. But there is no such method, nor is there any shortcut when it comes to character development. The process is individual, and what one person has to unlearn, another person might have to learn.

In spite of the uniqueness of each person's process, I believe we can learn from the process others have walked through and the principles they have applied. This book is my attempt to shed light on the refining process experienced by a wide variety of leaders and role models. Through our interviews and their own writings, these people were willing to share their experiences and give insight into how they persevered through dark seasons in their lives and dealt with obstacles without losing sight of their vision. Their experiences shed some light on the process that every dream chaser, every history maker, and every person seeking to pursue their destiny will experience: a training for reigning in the sphere they are destined to influence.

I invite you to join me on a journey into the hearts and minds of amazing men and women of courage, strength, faith, perseverance, and character. I pray that you will discover within these stories truths that you can apply to your own process. In the film *Shadowlands*, based on the life of C. S. Lewis, Lewis has a conversation with one of his students and says to him, "We read to know we are not alone." My hope is that, through reading this book, you will know you are not alone and will understand your own circumstances better. The insights from these people are worth more than gold and have the potential to transform your own personal struggle into a gateway of hope.

Chapter Two
Winning the Battle
of the Mind

Defeating the giant of toxic thinking

Les Brown

I found that most people fail in life not because they aim too high and miss. Most people fail in life because they aim too low and hit. And the majority of people don't aim at all.

Les Brown

Les Brown was born, along with his twin brother, on the floor of an abandoned building in a poor section of Miami, Florida, called Liberty City. At six weeks old they were adopted by Mrs Mamie Brown, a single black domestic worker. This woman had no more than a basic education, but she possessed a "PhD" in motherhood. Unable to have any children of her own, she ultimately adopted seven abandoned children, believing that somehow God would make a way for her to provide for them.

As Les grew up, his mother worked for the wealthy residents in Miami Beach, and she often took the children along and gave them chores to do. The first time she took Leslie into one of those beautiful mansions, he stared in amazement.

"Mama, why don't we live in a house like this?" he asked.

"Son, we can't afford to," she explained.

Les and his siblings often wore hand-me-down clothes from the families his mother worked for. If they were too long, his mom would hem them. If they were too short, she would let them out. They also often ate the leftover food from the meals she would cook in the rich people's homes.

Leslie often accompanied his mother to the house of one particular wealthy family. While there, he would find an excuse to slip into the owner's office – to empty the ashtray or dust the books. There he would linger while the owner listened to recorded messages by the writer and speaker Earl Nightingale. Young Les listened as Nightingale explained that we become what we focus our minds on. "You have greatness in you!" he would hear Nightingale declare. As Les kept hearing these words, they began to affect how he thought and how he saw himself. His vision of himself and what God could do with and through him began to expand. Nightingale's messages brought him to a new level of awareness that what he could do in life was greater than what he was experiencing at that time.

One day, after one of his cleaning and listening sessions in the owner's office, Les declared to his mom, "Mama! When I'm a man, I'm going to buy you a home *just like this*!"

"You don't have to buy me a home," she replied, wondering how this idea had even entered her son's mind.

"I know I don't have to. But I *want* to!"

There it was – the initial dream that Les Brown would pursue for the next two decades of his life. Later, he would embrace the idea of helping people all over the world discover the greatness God had placed within them. But the dream journey began with his mother. She had adopted him and given everything to take care of him, and thus as a young boy he decided that one day he was going to take care of her.

The battle of the mind

There was just one problem. Les didn't have the natural capacity to make the kind of money needed to buy his mother a mansion like the ones he had seen. Besides being born into poverty, he didn't see how he could climb that ladder of success through education, because he had been labelled as Educable Mentally Retarded (EMR). He failed third grade twice. Then, when he was in the eighth grade, he had to go back to grade seven. He was called the "DT" – the *dumb twin*. His brother Wesley was the smart one.

Every time Les was in the rich man's office listening to messages about the untapped potential and greatness within him, his heart would respond to the truth spoken over him. Deep inside, he believed that God had a greater destiny for him than what he was experiencing at that time. `but as soon as he walked out the door, his mind would take over and question his ability to do what he held in his heart. "And how do you think you are going to accomplish your dream, Les? How?!" As he listened to this negative internal dialogue that had been programmed into him, he became discouraged.

Today, Les Brown has a powerful message of hope, along with the ability to create a collective shift in thinking in any audience he speaks to. He has spoken to large corporations, organizations, and churches, as well as youth groups and prisoners, all over the world. He's even served as a state legislator in Ohio. People love his personality and his authenticity – and most of all his laughter. He has the gift of enabling his audience to discover the truth of who they are, and helping them believe that their lives can be changed and transformed.

Now, when he gets up to share this message, it is easy for him to do so. But the most difficult hurdle for Les to overcome – and it took him years to do it – was to believe that he was capable of doing what he does today; that he could be a messenger of hope, inspiration, and change. For a long time he did not believe it, and he silenced himself for more than fourteen years before he began to pursue his dream and rise above his circumstances.

The negative internal voices were a major obstacle that Les had to overcome in the early stages of walking out more of his potential and dream. This is also true for many, if not most, of us. Looking back, Les can see that his negative mindset kept him in bondage and did not allow the person we can see today to show up. He had to go through a major paradigm shift to get rid of the toxic thoughts about himself and his circumstances.

The book of Romans gives this admonition on the subject: "And do not be conformed to this world, but be transformed by the renewing of your mind" (Romans 12:2). This Scripture, which is one of Les's most frequently used quotes, describes the first process he had to go through. He knew that he was living an average life, but deep inside he had the potential to do more, to experience more, and to have a greater impact. The dream was knocking on the door of his heart every day, but his mind and fears silenced it for more than a decade.

Of course, the question at hand is how he managed to do it. How did Les Brown renew his mind and change his way of thinking? How did he break the negative messages that had been programmed into his subconscious mind and were inhibiting his progress in pursuing his dream and true potential? The answer is one we may not like to hear: to disrupt all that negative internal self-talk took a prolonged period of deliberate daily effort to fill his mind with the truth about himself.

Uncovering greatness

When speaking to large audiences about stepping into their destiny, Les Brown often shares a story of an event during his adolescence that impacted him greatly. One day at school Les was waiting in a classroom for his brother Wesley to arrive when the teacher, Mr Leroy Washington, called him to the front and said, "Go solve this problem for me."

"Sir," Les stuttered, "I can't do that, sir."

"Why not?" Mr Washington wanted to know.

"I'm not one of your students, sir."

"Go to the board and work the problem out anyhow," he replied.

"Oh, I can't do that, sir."

"Why not?"

"Because I am educable mentally retarded. I'm in special education."

At this point, the other students started laughing and yelling, "That's Leslie! He's not Wesley! He's the DT! Wesley is the smart twin!"

Mr Washington asked, "What does DT mean?"

"I'm the dumb twin, sir," Les admitted ruefully.

As the rest of the students burst out laughing, Mr Washington stood up behind his desk, walked over to stand in front of Les, looked deep into his eyes, and said with a stern voice, "Don't you ever say that again! *Someone else's opinion of you does not have to become your reality!*"

Mr Washington's words created a major interruption in the story that Les had believed to be true about himself. This was a very significant encounter, but it took more than just one incident to bring about a sustained change in his thinking. For Les, the long process of breaking through the negative voices in his life and developing the belief that he could become what he is today was, as described in Psalm 84:6, a valley of weeping, but he made it a spring of hope.

During his journey toward his dream, Les dealt not only with his own negative self-talk, but also with negative input from other people. When he announced that he was going to be a speaker, training people in organizations and corporations, his brother questioned him with an edge of cynicism in his voice.

"Les, do you have a college degree?"

"No, I don't," he replied.

"Les, do these people have PhDs and college degrees?"

"Yes, they do."

"Then how are you, Les Brown, going to train *them* and speak to *them*? How?!"

This process of renewing the mind, as the book of Romans describes it, concerns not only the cognitive level, but also the heart and emotional level. The whole inner being needs to be transformed. The word "mind" in this Scripture passage is not the optimal translation for the concept it expresses. The Hebrew understanding includes the heart, the emotions, the will, and the core of our being. Other Scriptures likewise refer to the *thoughts of the heart* (see, for example, Genesis 6:5; 1 Chronicles 29:18; Psalm 33:11; Matthew 15:19).

In recent years, neuroscientists have found that the heart has its own brain and is deeply connected to our thought processes.[1] And the thoughts that originate in the heart are particularly strong. Often, in the case of past experiences of brokenness and trauma, renewing the mind requires deep inner emotional healing before a change of mindset can take place. Chapter nine will offer more insight into that process.

The change of our thought patterns is an integral part of the refining process on our way to fulfilling our dreams and destiny. Nineteenth-century author Wallace D. Wattles points this out as the first, but most difficult, step: "To think according to appearances is easy. To think truth regardless of appearances is laborious and requires the expenditure of more power than any other workman is called upon to perform."[2] He adds that there is no other work that people avoid more than that of sustained thoughts of truth.

When life doesn't make sense

Today, to continue to combat the negative internal voices about his lack of ability or the obstacles he is facing, Les practices a regimen of daily routines to feed his mind with positive input.

For him, this means starting his day by listening to uplifting messages for at least half an hour, praying, meditating on the truth of Scripture, and speaking it over his life. In addition to that, he reads at least forty pages of something positive and inspiring every day, and he consciously shuts out any negative influences, whether from the news, from strangers, or from "friends".

As it would be for most people, this has been an extremely challenging process for Les, but it has yielded great results. More than anything else, it prepared him to stand firm in the midst of the most painful season in his life, which he faced some years later.

At the time, Les was running an awareness campaign to encourage men to have a prostate examination. The director of the campaign asked him if he had ever had an examination himself. When Les said he hadn't, the director challenged him to do so. Les took it to heart and soon visited his doctor.

Three days after his examination, he received a phone call from the doctor's office.

"Can you come in? We need to talk," the doctor said.

"No, I can't. What is it?" Les replied, noticing the difference in the doctor's voice.

"You have prostate cancer."

Although this unexpected news came as a blow, it didn't throw Les off course. He took it on as a project, like taking up a battle, and he was determined to win. It was actually another doctor's report – about his mother – that he received shortly after his own diagnosis that made him crumble. He was told that she had breast cancer, which had metastasized to the liver and other organs, and the doctors gave her only a few months to live.

"I still remember the day we received the doctor's report. I was with her to support her – but when the doctor gave us the news, I broke down crying. I thought I was the strong one, but I wasn't prepared for that," Les shared in our interview. "In the end, it was my mother and sister who supported me when we were walking out of the doctor's office."

One reason why this hit Les so hard was the special relationship he had with his mother. He says, "They always called me Mamie's boy, because even though I'm not her biological son, I have the same personality she did." Les's mother was always very uplifting, positive, fun-loving, and full of faith. "No matter what I was going through, she would always instil the faith in me that everything was going to turn out all right," Les explains.

She was his hero. So, upon receiving the news of her diagnosis, Les resigned from his office as a state representative and joined his siblings to take care of his mother.

Seeing his mother's health deteriorate to the point where she was completely incapacitated was one of Les's most difficult personal struggles. "She had been such a strong force in my life. She was a rock who had always been there for me," Les shares. "To be there, seeing her suffer and watching her take her last breath, was such a painful experience." He can still vividly recall sitting beside her bed and holding her lifeless hand, thinking about what kind of woman this was who had decided to take in children who weren't hers and to give her life to them. "She was a mystery to me, and I loved her and admired her. To process her suffering and death was the toughest challenge I have encountered in my life."

This was also a time of a fierce battle of emotions within Les. Anger rose within him because he was not able to stop her suffering. "I was angry with God that she had to go out that way; that she was in so much pain. And I was angry that there was nothing I could do to stop it. After a certain amount of medication, the doctors won't give any more pain relief, even if the patient is in pain. It was a painful death, and I couldn't stop it. I remember praying to God, asking him, 'Give it to me; I'm strong. I can beat it. But don't let my mother suffer.'" But he couldn't cut such a deal.

The morning after his mother had passed away, an article in a newspaper triggered a torrent of pain and anger in him. It reported that a mafia leader, who had been responsible for a large number of mob executions, had died comfortably in his sleep at ninety-two years of age in Miami. "At that moment, I became very angry," Les recalls. "This man had caused so much harm and suffering, but he had died comfortably in his sleep at ninety-two, yet my mother suffered terrible pain when she took her last breath."

What helped Les process his mother's suffering and deal with the anger and emotional turmoil? "It was the example of Shadrach, Meshach, and Abednego, who said, 'My God is able to deliver us from your hands, but even if he doesn't, we still won't bow,'" Les says (referring to Daniel 3:17–18). "I had to come to a place where I said, 'God, I know you're able to deliver her from this experience, but if you don't deliver her from this pain, if you don't bring her out of this experience, I still will not bow to anger, to depression, or to despair. I decided instead to focus on the years that God had blessed me with her life, with her love, and with her presence."

Believing against outward appearances

Through this and other experiences, Les has established a rule that he follows when dealing with life's difficult seasons: he guards his heart and refuses to allow it to become bitter. "Sooner or later we all encounter ordeals in life that do not make sense," Les shares. "Sometimes life doesn't happen the way we want it to happen, even with all of our prayers, with our tithing, and with all the good things we do."

But it is in this place of pain and suffering that the testing comes, and we must conquer the enemy inside. Les has built a foundation to stand on when storms hit. "I know that whatever I'm going through can make me bitter, or it can make me better," he says. "In life, you will always be faced with this series of God-ordained opportunities brilliantly disguised as problems and challenges – and when the very foundation of your life has been shaken, you run to God, only to discover that it is God who is doing this shaking."

Les emphasizes that we must remember God is there even if we are going through pain, and even if the situation is the opposite of what we think it should be. "I believe that God is in the midst of it, and that it is going to turn out all right. We must not judge according to outward appearances."

When we experience suffering and pain, our hearts are always challenged. For Les, dealing with disappointments and contradictions starts with a decision to trust God and to deliberately focus on his thought processes. Les says that in everything he is facing, he reminds himself that there is a way through. "I don't need to understand everything or make sense of it; what I need to do is to be grounded within myself and to know that my God is able to bring me through, that I am not dealing with this by myself. I need to remind myself that God is with me, even though I've made some requests that have not been answered."

After going through the experience of losing his mother, the focus of his prayers shifted. He no longer asks God to change circumstances, but instead he asks for strength to cope and to come out on the other side still believing, still loving, still trusting.

Not only did this critical experience change his relationship with God and his outlook on life; it also launched Les into his ultimate assignment, which has changed people's lives all over the world. "I decided that I was going to become more committed to making a difference, because even though my mother only had a very basic education, she made a difference in so many people's lives," Les shares. "A reporter once asked my mother what made her decide to adopt children. She said she wanted to share her life and make a difference. So she decided that she was going to make a difference in other people's lives – like she made a difference in mine. She put her stamp on me. She had a passion for love. She had a great sense of humour, and she loved and embraced people. I wanted to live my life like that. I wanted to be the kind of person who would touch people in a special way, as she touched me; who would love people, and who would help them see the possibilities of living their life to the fullest."

Destined to win

This is what Les Brown is doing to this day: impacting people's lives, encouraging them to follow their dreams, bringing change to the way they see themselves, and pointing them to the greatness they carry inside. One reason why he has such a powerful impact on people's lives is that he, the messenger, lives and embodies the message he teaches.

He lived this out in his battle with cancer. Every day for more than nineteen years after his diagnosis, he fought his cancer, speaking Scriptures and healing over himself. Every day he would say, "God, I give thanks that I am healed, that my immune system is strong and produces white blood cells, and will kill every renegade cancer cell in my body! I declare that every day and in every way I'm getting better and better." He did this for *nineteen years* and he did not neglect it for one single day. "I could not afford to!" Les emphasizes.

In 2013, Les received the doctor's report that his cancer had metastasized into his bones. He soon needed to wear pain patches, because the cancer had eaten into 40 per cent of his T1 vertebrae. He also had to wear a corset to support his spine. In spite of all that, he continued to thank God for healing, and publicly declared on stage that he was determined to win the battle and not bow to cancer.

He supports his approach with an article by Harvard medical researcher Dr Borysenko, who stated that no disease is incurable. According to Borysenko, all diseases can be cured, but most people are not willing to do the work. This work involves creating new neural pathways in your brain and speaking to your body on the cellular level. Les concurs: "Life and death are in the power of the tongue [Proverbs 18:21], and so often we speak death before we speak life." He continues, "You have to be in alignment with your thoughts, your vision, your words, your feelings, and your actions. You have to feel that it is done."

Seeing beyond cancer

When Les read the article, he determined to do the work. He decided that he would do whatever it took. "I saw myself beyond cancer. That's the capacity of imagination. God said to Abraham, 'I'll give you all your eyes can see' [Genesis 13:14–15]. The doctors determine the diagnosis, but God determines the prognosis – and that prognosis needs to become your reality. I had to see myself beyond cancer," Les affirms. He wants to see his great-grandchildren grow up. "Thirty years from now I will be here to go to my great-grandson's graduation. That is my mindset, and I work on that."

And so it was that one day, after nineteen years of speaking against the pain and declaring that he would not bow to it, Les began to feel his pain subside. This was in 2014. A CT scan done shortly afterward left his doctors amazed. "We don't know what happened or what you did. But you can go and live your life. You are free of cancer," they said.

"I know God spared my life for the greater purpose and assignment of helping people discover the greatness in themselves, to raise up voices of hope in the world that impact their nations and become agents of change. And I am committed to that cause," Les reflects. Working on his mindset took diligence and perseverance, but it has helped him stand strong through the ups and downs of life and to hold the course in the midst of the storms.

As much as this would be a desirable ending for this chapter, it is not the end of the story. Life often takes unexpected turns, and so it did with Les: in 2016 the storm rose up again when he found out that the cancer had returned. The diagnosis, however, hasn't changed his approach to life, his beliefs, or his daily practice of working on his mindset. He has his mind fixed on his goal and works every day at keeping it renewed. He continues to declare that he will not judge according to appearances, circumstances, or doctors' reports, but according to a higher standard: the truth that sets him free.

Les Brown is an outstanding example of someone who has built a strong anchor to remain grounded and weather the storms of life. He is not swayed by circumstances, and, even in the midst of his own battles, he always has up words for down times. Whenever he gets on the stage and speaks, his words pierce the souls of his listeners. He holds up his testimony like a mirror that reflects what is possible for those who believe. His example invites you to embark on the journey of faith, of refusing to bow to circumstances, and of discovering the greatness within you. It's never too late, and, as his example shows, it's worth the effort!

Chapter Three
Camped at the Gates of Hell

The test of perseverance

Rolland and Heidi Baker

To turn faith into a personal possession is a
fight always, not sometimes. God brings us into
circumstances in order to educate our faith, because
the nature of faith is to make its object real.

Oswald Chambers

When Rolland and Heidi Baker first set off for Mozambique in 1995, the whole country was dealing with the aftermath of decades of civil war. People were blowing up relief vehicles, vandalizing, looting, and fighting for survival. Floods, famine, and diseases were ravaging the country. In certain communities, AIDS had wiped out nearly an entire generation, leaving children as orphans and once-populated villages as ghost towns. The atmosphere was depressing, hopeless, and dire. It felt like the most godforsaken place on earth. But Rolland and Heidi Baker believed it was the perfect place to bring hope to the hopeless, to shine God's love in the midst of darkness, and to see the kingdom of God invade and transform the direst circumstances.

They were compelled by a vision: they wanted to see the teaching of the Sermon on the Mount become a reality among the most grief-stricken, suffering people they could find on earth. They wanted to go to Mozambique to put the truth of the gospel to the test. They sought to heal the sick, raise the dead, and see people set free from trauma, wounds, and demonic oppression. And they wanted to learn from the poorest of the poor about the kingdom of God (Matthew 5:3).

By this time, Rolland and Heidi had been missionaries in Indonesia, China, and England for more than twenty years, but, having seen little fruit from years of hard work, they had become tired.

What, then, made them decide that going into one of the darkest places on earth would be better? It was a holy frustration. Rolland had once tasted and experienced the reality of the gospel in a dark place. Years before, he had seen what was possible, and now he was no longer willing to settle for less.

Visions beyond the veil

Rolland had grown up as a third-generation missionary kid in Kunming, China. His grandfather Harold Baker had pioneered a work there in the early 1900s. Together with his wife Josephine, Harold had taken in street children of a particular kind: those considered the scum of society, the orphans nobody wanted, the rascals, gang members, and criminals. These were the street kids that other Christians had warned them not to take in, for they considered them hopeless and a waste of time. But the Bakers took them into their home, the Adullam Rescue Center, where they loved them, provided for them, and prayed for them.

The children, primarily boys aged between six and eighteen, were challenging and difficult from the start. Their hearts were wounded, their spirits were crushed, and they kept reverting to their criminal lifestyle. Harold and Josephine persevered in patience, love, and prayer, and one day God broke through. The boys began to have spiritual encounters. They suddenly saw visions of Jesus, of angels and demons, of heaven and hell.

Their hearts were changed and filled with the revelation of spiritual truths that should have required years of theological training to understand. Later, these children, once considered scum, became significant leaders in their society. This amazing story, known as the Adullam Revival, is recounted in H. A. Baker's book *Visions Beyond the Veil*.

Growing up in China, Rolland was greatly influenced by the faith and testimony of his grandfather. But after returning to America as an adolescent and then attending seminary, he experienced little of life in the Spirit. Even worse, he began to hear that the Sermon on the Mount didn't really mean what he thought it meant. He was taught that healing the sick, raising the dead, doing greater works than Jesus, trusting God for daily provision, which he so longed to experience in his own life, weren't realistic in today's society. The answers he received from teachers, churches, and theologians created a holy frustration within Rolland.

But then he met Heidi.

Compelled by love

Heidi grew up in a wealthy home on a private beach in California. She had a privileged upbringing and lacked for nothing in education, comforts, or opportunities. But, even as a young girl, a deep compassion for the needy consumed her. That passion first manifested itself in her collection of homeless animals from the neighbourhood. She drove her parents nuts when she turned their property into an animal shelter and took in pet number thirty-two. They called their young daughter's habit a "compassion tic", but they had no idea how big it would become in her adult life.

In addition to Heidi's childhood gift of compassion, a deep hunger for God stirred inside of her. She was raised in the Anglican tradition, but at the age of sixteen she had an experience that would change her life forever. That summer, she spent three months volunteering on an Indian reservation. There, during an ordinary church service, as she listened to a Navajo pastor preach, Heidi had a divine encounter. She experienced a vivid vision of Jesus, and she was totally undone by his love and compassion.

When she returned home, she announced to her parents that she had received a vision of Jesus and was planning to become a missionary in Asia, England, and Africa. They thought she had lost her mind. With all their might, they made every effort to bring her "back to her senses". One day, her mother, desperate to get Heidi to return to her "normal life", served her "space cookies" (cookies baked with marijuana) to get her stoned and dissuade her from preaching at a youth meeting.

But Heidi was single-minded in her embrace of the vision, and began sharing the gospel whenever she had the opportunity. She began to go on mission trips where she trusted Jesus for everything without question, and expected God to lead and provide. Her love for people, and especially for the unlovely, flowed naturally and without effort.

When Rolland met Heidi in a small church and listened to her testimony, she became to him a living fulfilment of the Sermon on the Mount, and especially the Beatitudes.[1] Rolland felt instantly drawn to Heidi and believed that she was a person with whom he could actually live out the Sermon on the Mount as he had always dreamed. Six months after they met, they were married. And two weeks after their wedding, they left for the mission field with simple instructions from God, one-way tickets, and thirty dollars in their pockets.

Back to basics

Heidi and Rolland served faithfully on the mission field – first for sixteen years in Asia, and then for another ten in England.

They walked in faith and devoted themselves to the work, but saw little of the desired move of God. Then, one day, Rolland read an article in *National Geographic* about Mozambique. He described it to Heidi, relating that Mozambique was the third-poorest country in the world and at the time was embroiled in civil war. He shared that people were even blowing up Red Cross relief trucks. Heidi immediately said, "Let's go there!"

So they did. It was 1995, and this time they took a new approach. They did not enter this mission field to *teach* about the kingdom of heaven. Instead, they went there to *learn* from the poor about the kingdom of God. Specifically, they wanted to know what the Beatitude in Matthew 5:3 meant: "Blessed are the poor in spirit, for theirs is the kingdom of heaven." By this point in their missionary career, they were desperate to see the truth of the gospel at work. In her book, *Compelled by Love*, Heidi writes, "If God was not with us in this unfamiliar world and ministry, we did not want to continue. If He could not be trusted and followed, if the Sermon on the Mount was simply impractical, if we could not do 'even greater things' than Jesus did (John 14:12), then our work was and still is hopeless."[2]

When Heidi arrived in Mozambique, she sat at a street corner in Maputo, watching and listening for instructions from God. Suddenly, she heard him ask, "Do you see these children?"

She did, because they were impossible to overlook. The area was full of children, most of them clothed in rags, scavenging for something to eat on the street and among the garbage.

"Take them home!" Heidi heard God's voice speak to her heart.

"God, I don't have a home," Heidi replied.

But she heard him say again, "Take these children home."

"God, I've just finished my PhD, and I want to work with adults. Children can't think. I don't do *children...*" she responded.

"Well, you do now!" she heard him say.

And so Heidi invited the children to go with her. But she didn't know where to take them.

As they waited on the street corner in Maputo for further instructions from God, a woman approached Heidi. This stranger told her to gather the children and follow her to her home.

Turning orphans into sons and daughters

That is how it all started. They had begun to take in some of the most challenging orphans: the kind of street kids other Christians considered a waste of time and warned them not to take in. Rolland and their children soon arrived to join Heidi in the work. They rescued children from the garbage dumps, from the street corners, from the brothels. They soon built a home to house everyone. Rolland and Heidi took the gospel literally and put it to the test. And they experienced the supernatural provision of God: his guidance, his power, and his miracles.

Today, their organization, Iris Ministries, is a beacon of light in Mozambique that has changed the atmosphere throughout the nation. Every day, Iris feeds thousands of children and adults, and provides medical aid, education, well-drilling, shelter, clothing... and, most of all, love. Iris children's centres turn orphans into sons and daughters who radiate hope and joy. The street kids Rolland and Heidi adopted when they began more than twenty years ago are now leaders – both within the ministry and in the country. Together they meet with government officials, hand out relief supplies, and help transform the nation.

Suffering and glory

But it hasn't always been that glorious. In the early years of their pioneer work, Rolland and Heidi faced extreme persecution from the Marxist government, because it suspected that Iris was collaborating with the rebels. The pressure from the government was so intense that most of their volunteers left.

"We had every destruction imaginable," Heidi recalls. "Rolland, our two blond children, and I had to escape in the middle of the night for our lives."

Government officials raided the centre. "Then they said to the children there that they could stay if they wouldn't pray and read the Bible any longer," she continues. "But all answered in unison that they would follow Jesus. Our children were beaten, had stones thrown at them, and they had to leave the centre."

Those children walked twenty-seven kilometres barefooted and found Heidi and Rolland in their little office in Maputo the following day. Now they had 100 children with no place to stay. Heidi says of that night, "We had all these children and no food left. Our money was gone. Our support was gone. And I was exhausted and angry. 'Why is this happening to us?' I was questioning. 'This is a disaster. There are all these children. There are no beds. There's no food. What are we supposed to do?' My faith hit rock bottom."

Then somebody knocked at the door. It was a woman from the American embassy who had heard about the Bakers' escape from the centre and came to offer some food that she had cooked for their family – their family of four.

Heidi thanked her, but then said, "But we have a huge family..." and showed her the 100 children in the back yard.

The woman gasped in shock and cried, "Oh no! There is only food for four! I didn't make enough!"

But Heidi just said, "Jesus died so that there's always enough."

"I didn't even think," Heidi says now. "It wasn't like I was full of faith. I was totally exhausted, and I had all these children to feed. So we prayed. We gave thanks for the food. We had a little bowl of cornmeal, some chilli, and rice. If you stretched it, it could have fed ten people at the most. Then I said to the woman, 'Let's give them a lot, because they are hungry.' That's when we experienced the first miracle of food multiplication.

"We had a few plastic bowls. I didn't know at that time that God could multiply plastic, but we started filling them up, and everybody ate, even the woman! She was crying by then because she had never seen a miracle."

That was just the first of many miracles that Iris Ministries would go on to experience on a regular basis. All of the amazing stories of God revealing himself through signs and wonders in the midst of the most dire and hopeless circumstances are recounted in Rolland and Heidi's book, *There Is Always Enough*.

In our Western world, few have seen such miracles of food multiplication or healing, and many who hear about them want to experience and see them with their own eyes. But what most people are not aware of is that the flip side of glory is suffering. It is usually in the midst of suffering, in devastation and destruction, that God breaks through in miraculous ways.

"In horrific times, miracles and revival are birthed," Heidi explains. "The revival in China came in the midst of great persecution. The revival in Mozambique came in the midst of great floods. We see food multiply all the time. God told me to feed the nations. There's always enough, because he died for us. So I just believe him and we feed the nations with spiritual and physical food."

Rolland's battle

That was in 1995. Fast-forward fourteen years to 2009. Heidi was teaching Westerners at their mission school in Pemba, Mozambique, about the cost of seeing a breakthrough and carrying the glory of God.

"It was hard back then," Heidi would explain to them when describing the pioneering stages of their work, but in the same breath she would continue, "It's harder now."

At the time, Rolland's life was hanging by a thread. After months of medical examinations and tests, his doctors had given up on him, saying there was nothing they could do. His diagnosis was indefinable, and the doctors were certain of only one thing: it was terminal.

"Your brain is shrinking," they told Rolland after examining one of the many MRI scans. "It's like the advanced stage of dementia – you have the brain of an old man," the white coats concluded.

Dr Rolland Baker, a brilliant man, was slowly losing his mind. He didn't know where he was any more, he couldn't recognize people any more, he couldn't dress himself any more. Drooling, he just lay in bed twenty-two hours a day.

His condition had started deteriorating drastically after a bout of cerebral malaria. Most of the time, however, one misfortune seldom comes alone, and this was the case with Rolland. "There were all kinds of issues that played into this situation," Heidi says. "He'd had a series of mini strokes, he was dealing with post-traumatic stress after coming back from Sudan where he had witnessed the most horrible atrocities, and he was working way too hard."

That's when the first signs of mental torment began to show, as Rolland experienced increasing restlessness, fear, and irritability. "In a strange way, that was a lot harder than when he had actually lost his mind," Heidi shares. "He couldn't sit still any more or relax. He was scared, pacing constantly, and freaking out all the time. He just couldn't receive peace." He began to shuffle like an old man.

Seeing her husband slowly deteriorate to a vegetative state was very painful for Heidi – but it was a hellish experience for Rolland himself. "It was an extremely tough fight," Rolland says now. "For two years, I felt like I was literally camped at the gates of hell." He heard demonic voices and could not silence them. They would harass him constantly, screaming that he wouldn't make it, that he didn't have enough faith, that he would not be able to hang on, that he would end up in hell, and that there was nothing he could do about it.

"I was scared, and I literally felt the flames of hell during that time," Rolland continues. "I felt extremely depressed and very claustrophobic, because I couldn't kick myself out of it. When you are in that place, nobody can get you out of it. There is no pill you can take, there is no counselling you can go to, there is no book you can read. Then you realize the only thing you have left is Jesus."

Up or down?

Through constant prayer and reading the Bible, Rolland tried to encourage himself, to strengthen his faith, and to fight the fear and mental torment. But there came a time when he couldn't read or pray any more. The only thing he could do was simply not give up.

"When things get really tough there are only two directions to go: up or down. That's it. You throw away your faith in Jesus and it's down," he says. "I really appreciate the book of Job. That's not a popular teaching these days, but I am convinced now more than ever that Job's experience is applicable to all Christians everywhere."

Many Christians argue that the book of Job belongs to the Old Testament and does not apply to new covenant believers, but Rolland points to the book of James, which says, "You have heard of the endurance of Job and have seen the outcome of the Lord's dealings, that the Lord is full of compassion and *is* merciful" (James 5:11, NASB).

Rolland says of Job's story, "After all his trials, he became twice as prosperous as before, had the most beautiful daughters in the land, and forever in heaven is glorified for being able to say, 'Though He slay me, yet will I trust Him [Job 13:15].'

That was my key to winning the battle," Rolland says. "You can hardly go through worse than Job, but once you decide to follow God, no matter what happens, you are free."

That was what Rolland knew he had to do. He had to decide to rust God even if he could not live through this. "Everyone should make up their mind about this when first becoming a Christian. Once you decide that, a lot of things are easier."

The perseverance test

Most crises in our lives are deep learning experiences. What Rolland learned during this intense battle was that a lot of preaching about the Christian life is clearly wrong.

"Large ministries are badly misleading people when they convey that being a Christian is like suddenly entering a bubble, that you will experience heaven on earth all the way, that you are not going to have to prove anything or develop any strength, be tested in any way, or be purified in any way," Rolland says. "That is not the thrust of the New Testament. Paul says in the book of Acts, 'Through many tribulations we enter the kingdom of heaven' [Acts 14:22]. Psalm 34:19 states that many are the afflictions of the righteous, but God delivers him out of them all. That's part of the Christian life, because it is that kind of strength and victory that glorifies God, not just being favoured and blessed. Many students coming out of ministry schools get extremely confused, because life is not happening the way they were taught."

When you have a dream and want to make a difference on earth, walking it out is not a stroll. God has laid out for us a race to run. The book of Hebrews encourages us to "run with endurance the race that is set before us" (Hebrews 12:1).

"Some people's race is easy, for some people it is harder, but for the great martyrs – the really great people of history – it was very hard. But the reward is much greater," Rolland says.

"And so you have to decide: is it up or down? There is no pill to take; there is nothing you can do to suddenly feel good. You have to persevere."

This also happened to the apostle Paul. He wrote to the believers in Corinth that he was under so much pressure that he despaired of life itself, he was perplexed, and thought he would die (2 Corinthians 1:8). But he also said that these things happen "that we might not rely on ourselves but on God, who raises the dead" (2 Corinthians 1:9, NIV UK).

"Paul was locked up in prison, and so was Joseph. They didn't know whether they would ever get out. But you don't have a choice but to persevere," Rolland emphasizes. "The only other option is just to give up and lose everything, and you can't do that. *The real test in suffering is persevering.* Jesus says, 'The one who endures to the end will be saved' [Matthew 24:13, NLT]."

Heidi's battle

While Rolland was going through this hellish experience – the greatest demonic attack on his life – Heidi had to carry sole responsibility for the ministry and organization. And in the two environments of ministry and home, she wrestled with the contradiction that she witnessed every day: the blind being healed, the lame walking, the deaf hearing... and her husband drooling, not knowing where he was.

"It was heartbreaking, and a lot of times I was just frustrated," Heidi shares. "There were times when I just said to God, 'Heal him or take him! Do one or the other. Don't just let this brilliant man waste away to nothing!' And there were times when I would just burst into tears when he couldn't figure out how to put on a shirt. There would be times when I would just sob when I watched him trying to put on flip-flops and he couldn't understand how to put his foot in. Other times I would take him out on outreach and he would just lie down in the dirt. That was really hard to see."

How did Heidi cope with it all and not give up? "I just had to lean totally on Jesus," she says. But leaning on God is something you only learn over time. "At times, getting to the place of leaning on God is a struggle, and at times it's just mere exhaustion," Heidi explains. "When you're exhausted and you're trying to stand, you sometimes lean on a wall or hold on to something. That's what leaning on Jesus means – you can't support yourself in your own strength any more. So you learn to lean on him. But now I also lean on him in the best of times. I don't just lean on Jesus when it's hard. He has become the source of my strength – my everything."

Deciding to love

Heidi had the additional burden of deciding what to do next. "There were all these decisions to make, and that felt like a weight. But what was actually really beautiful to see was that the very children we had picked up from the garbage dump and the street corners poured out their love on Rolland in this time. When I was speaking somewhere or was out in the bush they would take care of him. They would feed him, wash him, and drive him around in his Land Rover. So it was an extremely hard and challenging time, but it was also bittersweet, because I saw so many people we loved pour out love back on him. Through this, God spoke to me clearly and said, 'Your job is to love; my job is to heal.'"

And he did. God healed Rolland. A community of believers with medical training in Germany offered to host and work with him. Heidi gratefully sent him there, where they cared for him spiritually, physically, emotionally, and medically.

"I don't know what did the trick," Rolland says now. "I received a lot of vitamins, freshly pressed juices, and holistic medical care. I took a lot of walks and hikes, and, most of all, I received a lot of love. People just sat with me and ministered to me."

At first, his improvement was gradual, but then it became much more rapid. Only a few months later, Rolland was back in Mozambique, flying the ministry aeroplane with supplies for the most unreached people groups in the nation.

The test of love

The prolonged battle over Rolland's life was extremely challenging, but Heidi's life has been at stake many times, too. "In the early stages of our work here in Mozambique she had blood poisoning, pneumonia, chronic fatigue syndrome, and something that looked like MS," Rolland says. She was shot at, had stones thrown at her, was hunted by the government, and was close to death many times.

Interestingly, the external oppression and health issues are not what Heidi considers to have been her most challenging trials. "The human aspect and the relationships are far more painful," she says. "We have been close to death many times, but the most challenging issue for me is when a child that we have taken in and poured love into turns on us, steals enormous amounts of money, or betrays us. Or when a missionary leaves the ministry or even turns away from God because a child beat them up and they are angry – that's hard. For me, the human conflicts are always far more painful," Heidi continues. "I have had some kids that have really fallen deep, but bar none they all come back. These are kids that have embezzled money, committed adultery, got drunk, slandered and tried to shut down the ministry, and then they come back saying, 'Mom, I love you so much.'"

She goes on, "This is where the love test comes in. Then I have to decide: am I going to embrace that son (it's usually a son) who is just so screwed up in every way? Am I going to love him and forgive him? That's the toughest test for me. It doesn't mean I'm going to trust him – at least not right away. I wouldn't hand over my credit card... But that's where the grace of God comes in, and I just think about what Jesus has done for me."

Forgiving a child who has betrayed them and stolen from them is a real love test. Being able to forgive the government and trying to work with and honour them is incredibly challenging. If you were to meet Heidi, this would surprise you, for she exudes an extraordinary love all around that draws people to her like a magnet. But the glory, the miracles, and the love she carries come with a price tag.

The biggest test of love: forgiving a parent

"My biggest love test – and this is probably true for most people – is forgiving a parent," Heidi shares. "I had a wonderful father, but my mother had really crazy mental episodes, and I never shared this until after she passed away." She continues, "I led my mother to the Lord, but before she got saved, she had a lot of horrific episodes. Once she even tried to kill me.

"I grew up really privileged. We had everything: we had ski trips, Mexico trips, private cello lessons, private ballet; we lived on a private beach. You name it. I loved horse riding and was already using a specific horse, so it was practically mine, but I was asking if I could have it. She yelled at me, 'You spoiled, selfish girl!' and dragged me into the car." As they raced along the rocky coast, Heidi began to realize that her mother intended to run the car off the cliff. "She was going to kill herself and me. I was totally petrified. This was beyond crazy and scary. I thought I was going to die. Just before they reached the cliff's edge, her mother stopped the car and started sobbing. Heidi didn't understand at the time, but she knows now that God stopped her mother. "Because I have been through inner healing, I now know that Jesus put his foot on the brake and took the wheel."

Heidi's difficult relationship with her mother coloured every aspect of her life, even after she became a Christian. "When

I became a Christian, I thought I had forgiven my mother," Heidi explains. "But one day God really pinned me down and said, 'You haven't really forgiven your mother.' I argued with him and said, 'Yes, I did!' But actually, I had not. And when I realized it, I really forgave her. After that, I was able to have a better relationship with Rolland, because subconsciously I had put the judgments I had on my mother on to Rolland, which made him act in a similar way at times. Through a whole process of forgiving, things began to change. I also developed a deeper relationship with Father God. My earthly dad was perfect in my eyes, but my mom was scary. Once I forgave my mom, I could really step into my identity as a daughter of God, as *Daddy's girl*."

Sons and daughters

Heidi is confident that becoming established in your identity as a son or daughter of God is key to facing the contradictions and challenging circumstances in life. We need to know who we are in God in order not to fall for the accusations that come from either the enemy or within. The first question most people ask themselves when they face difficult times is, "What have I done wrong?" Many Christians still live under the mistaken notion that when you are right with God, blessings will follow, but when tragedy hits, it is a sign that you did something wrong. But often, instead of analyzing ourselves, we need to lean on God. What we need in difficult times is confidence to enter into the presence of God and find help in time of need (see Hebrews 4:14–15).

Rolland says that one of the most important things we need to understand in our Christian lives is the atonement – what Christ has done for us, and who we really are in God's sight. "I have met a lot of people who, after they made a big mistake, got tempted and sinned, or just went off and did something else, have a very hard time forgiving themselves and approaching God again. They think they have failed him and ruined their lives. Satan is the accuser. He is the one suggesting that there is no hope, that we blew it, or that God doesn't accept us any more. But we know that he loves us and that he will give us grace, because he died for us."

This understanding of the atonement has been the foundation of their trust in difficult times. Rolland continues, "Because he died, there is always enough. His miracles, his provision, and his resources are without end! There is always enough grace, enough forgiveness, enough healing, enough love. There is always enough to meet every need of his sons and daughters, and he does it not sparingly, but according to his *glorious riches*."

Rolland and Heidi, through steadfastness and exercising their faith, have seen with their own eyes and experienced in their own lives that there is always enough. God's abundance is available, but the key to making the object of your faith real, according to early twentieth-century evangelist Oswald Chambers, whom I quoted at the beginning of this chapter, is persevering in faith in times of contradictions and totally depending on God. Rolland and Heidi have endured the scorching heat of prolonged desert experiences in their lives, but they have never allowed their well of hope to run dry. As a result, they have turned this faith, that Jesus has made provision for us in every way and for every circumstance, into a personal possession. The Sermon on the Mount continues to be real in their lives.

Chapter Four:
The X Factors

The test of unreserved surrender

Loren Cunningham

You have to decide what your highest priorities are and
have the courage to say "no" to other things. And the
way you do that is by having a bigger "yes" burning
inside. The enemy of the "best" is often the "good".

Stephen R. Covey

He was slowly pulling up the driveway of Aunt Sandra and
Uncle George's grand summer house in Lake Placid,
New York. The white façade of the mansion reflected on
the glassy surface of the water drew him toward the stately
home. The weather was gorgeous and a fresh breeze from
the lake welcomed him as he stepped out of his old, non-air-
conditioned Chevy.

He took a deep breath and strolled to the lakeside, taking
in the magnificent view of the mountainous landscape in the
background and the tranquillity of his immediate surroundings.
He stretched under the shade of the trees and walked back to
the driveway. He was struck by how dingy his old Chevy with
peeling metallic blue paint looked right next to Aunt Sandra's
brand new Cadillac.

He had to admit he had an appreciation for quality things.
Aunt Sandra and Uncle George moved in a glamorous world
that was far removed from his own. It was a good feeling to be

here in these surroundings, riding in Aunt Sandra's Cadillac and even driving it occasionally. And all of this could be his. He would just have to say "yes" to their offer.

"Loren, darling!" Aunt Sandra kissed him on the cheek, took him by the arm, and walked him to the garden. "I'm so glad you could make it and come to see us! There's something your uncle and I are anxious to discuss with you in the morning."

Loren Cunningham knew what it was they wanted to discuss. He was sure it was a job offer – and it would be a *very good* job.

Later, after dinner, Loren retreated to his room to take some time alone and process what was about to happen the next morning and consider the answer he would have to give.

Vision of waves

That night he was restless, twisting in the silk sheets and peering out at the moonlit sky. He could see the stars from his window. His thoughts went back to the vision he had received during a mission trip to the Bahamas six years earlier. He could still see the picture in his mind's eye: waves flooding the shores of every nation and suddenly turning into young people. They covered the shores of every continent, every country of the globe. He was perplexed at the time and rubbed his eyes, yet still he saw the waves of people. "What is this?" he wondered back then. Was that God speaking to him?

He had concluded that the vision was real, but now, at Aunt Sandra's house, he found himself struggling again. "Was that really you, Lord?" he asked once more. He needed to know for sure that he would not be throwing away the opportunity of a lifetime to take over a multimillion-dollar business based on a vain imagination or a ludicrous vision he had conjured up himself.

But the vision didn't let him go. He still felt the burning desire that it had given him: to see young people released into missions, into making a difference in people's lives, and into bringing the good news to the poor. This went completely against what he'd been taught as he'd been growing up in a traditional church system: that people could only be released into mission work after years of theological training. The vision gave Loren an assurance that the potential and passion within young people could be released in a mighty way if only they were given the opportunity to step out and show the love of God to different people groups and nations.

The vision of waves covering every continent and every nation had taken hold of him – and that night he knew he had to take hold of it in the same way. Deep inside he knew this was his life's calling, his mission, his destiny: releasing young people all over the world to bring the good news to the entire world. But how would he tell Aunt Sandra and Uncle George?

A decision to follow the call of God had once before created a rift in his family and had caused Aunt Sandra to turn away from Christianity. This made it all the more difficult for Loren to tell her about his call to the mission field, even though the trouble had occurred many years before Loren was born.

Loren's grandfather owned a successful laundry business in the early 1900s when he received his "call" to preach. He immediately sold the business and followed his call, preaching part-time and working part-time to support his wife and their five children – among them Aunt Sandra and Loren's dad, Tom. Then, during the smallpox epidemic of 1916, tragedy struck. Several members of the family came down with the disease. All recovered save one: the children's mother. Loren's grandfather was left to raise five young children – three girls and two boys. For the children, the trauma of their mother's death was already great, but the tragedy went to a new level for them when their father announced that he had heard a call from God to be a full-time travelling preacher.

In order to follow his call right away, he decided that rather than taking five children with him on the road he would separate them and place each one in the home of a different friend, who took them in for the chores they could do. Today, we see the cruelty of this decision, but to him it seemed like a good solution, partly because back then it was believed that children were well taken care of if they had a roof over their heads and three meals a day. In reality, the children felt isolated and abandoned.

The Cunningham children each dealt very differently with their father's decision and the negative impact it had on their childhood. Loren's dad Tom ended up following in his father's footsteps and becoming a preacher himself, but some of the other children had a much harder time. In fact, Sandra and one other sister responded by rejecting Christianity altogether.

Looking back on the story recounted by his family, Loren believes that his grandfather made a serious mistake in his interpretation of God's calling. "Hearing God is not at all difficult," Loren writes in his book *Is That Really You, God?* "But we can hear His voice once and still miss His best if we don't keep on listening. After the *what* of guidance come the *when* and *how*."[1] He believes his granddad had heard the *what*, but failed to seek further guidance and wisdom about the *when* and the *how*. Had he sought God for wisdom on the manner and timing of the calling, Loren believes that much of the resulting pain for his children might have been prevented.

Unfortunately, Sandra and her sister blamed their difficult childhood on their father's call itself, so they wanted nothing to do with religion. But they still loved their siblings. So later, when they had become successful in business, they offered to pay for their younger brother Tom to pursue a college degree in engineering. They were appalled when he said he wanted to study to become a preacher. The sisters viewed a religious career as an excuse to live off the charity of others. They delivered an ultimatum: if Tom chose the same path as their father had, they would have nothing more to do with him. And that is exactly what happened.

Many years passed. Tom's son Loren was born and grew up not knowing his Aunt Sandra at all. He prayed for many years for family reconciliation. Then, when he was twenty, a mission trip to the Caribbean took him through New York, where Aunt Sandra lived. He contacted her to ask if they could meet, and she agreed to do so. When they met, she took an immediate liking to him. They agreed to keep in touch. To Loren, it felt as though she wanted their connection as a way to make up for the lost years with her brother Tom.

That night, as he lay in bed in the guest room of Aunt Sandra's house, Loren felt the weight of the conversation that would come the next morning. He knew his aunt intended to make him a great offer – similar in magnitude to the one she had made to his dad. He also knew, based on his clear vision, that he would have to decline, just as his father had, and tell her he had been called to be a missionary. Would this again cause a tear in the family? These thoughts weighed heavily on him.

The splendid offer

Loren hardly slept a wink. Finally, after a night of tossing and turning in the darkened room, he looked at his watch. Nine o'clock. He rang for the butler, who appeared moments later bearing a breakfast tray loaded with all his favourites: ripe melon, waffles, eggs, bacon, and a tall glass of freshly squeezed orange juice. Loren did his best to enjoy his meal, then half-heartedly dressed and walked downstairs to find his aunt waiting for him on the terrace.

"Loren! Good morning, dear! How did you sleep?"

"Fine," he said, glancing away.

"Come, take a seat," Aunt Sandra said. "Loren, we're so

glad you were able to come. We've been anxious to ask if you would consider coming to work with Uncle George..."

Here it was. The question he knew he had to answer; the moment he had come to fear. He really cared for his aunt, and he understood all too well the generosity of her and his uncle's invitation. What they were offering was a chance to become part of their multimillion-dollar family business – like a son, an heir.

Loren took a deep breath. "It isn't that I don't marvel at what you've offered me, Aunt Sandra," he began.

"But you're saying no – is that it?" she probed.

Quickly, he tried to describe how he had heard a call to preach when he was thirteen, and then, in his twenties, God had spoken to him – this time by showing him the vision of waves of young people taking the good news to every continent of the world. The words felt awkward coming out of his mouth. He writes, "Somehow though, as I heard my voice telling her about my vision, it sounded presumptuous."[2]

Good is the enemy of best

His aunt tried to argue that he could do ministry within the United States – that there were plenty of people right there who needed help. Looking at her face, Loren saw the worry and concern, and a knife twisted inside him. He hated letting her down, but he knew he had to put this test behind him. He cleared his throat and found his voice.

"I can't, Aunt Sandra. I just cannot accept your offer. It's to the whole world that God has called me, and I have to obey."

As they talked, it was clear that she didn't really understand, but Loren was relieved that she ultimately respected his decision. This time, a calling would not lead to a family rift. Aunt Sandra told him that she would do her best to explain his decision to Uncle George. At that point, the only thing he could do was bid her farewell. So he said goodbye, turned, and walked through the big double doors, down the wide marble stairs and away from an amazing offer. This test was over.

As Loren drove away, he determined to stay close to Aunt Sandra and her family, and at the same time stay true to his calling. Now, as he drove over the bridge toward the airport, he wondered about the waves and his next steps. He had six volunteers to help with his vision – hardly waves. But now that he had passed this test, surely great doors would open and God would reward his obedience – right?

Not quite. Instead, this would only be the first in a series of tests of surrender to the call that Loren would have to pass. In the following months, he continued to give feet to the vision. Together with his wife Darlene and the few volunteers, he organized the first project for their fledgling organization: Youth With A Mission (YWAM). Eventually, they boarded a plane with 100 young people to travel to the Bahamas, the Caribbean, and South America to preach the gospel.

During this trip his vision began to take more shape. The young people did a great job of sharing the gospel. But when a terrible hurricane hit the islands and destroyed the homes of thousands of people, it became clear to Loren that bringing the gospel was more than just preaching words. He recognized that the love of God needed to be demonstrated and made known to the people in meaningful ways. Love looks like something – and the love of God needed to be made real in the direst of circumstances. Loren found himself wondering, "Wouldn't it be great if we had a ship with medical equipment and provisions to dock on every island, to help rebuild houses, provide food and medical care, and meet the people where they feel the greatest needs?" He continued pondering this thought.

Painful separation

News about the great success of the young people's outreach in the Bahamas and Caribbean islands travelled fast and preceded Loren's meeting with his superior where he was employed as a pastor. Before the meeting, Loren anticipated a great collaboration, where he would be released to follow his vision. His dream was actually working! And he was excited that YWAM had opened the doors for all denominations, although he still wanted to stay within the framework of his church organization. As he travelled to the denominational headquarters, he was looking forward to the meeting.

But Loren was mistaken. In the meeting, his superior told him immediately that he would have to limit his future missions teams to no more than ten young people if he wanted to continue to operate within the framework of the denomination. Plus, Loren's idea of making this an *interdenominational* youth outreach organization was not an option at all. His supervisor went on to assure him that he could continue to receive a fine salary and take small teams of young people here and there to other continents – but Loren knew that this would be a mere trickle compared to the vision of waves God had shown him.

"My heart dropped to my knees as the very gracious offer came out – it sounded so reasonable, so secure. Only it was far from what I believed God had told me to do," Loren writes in his book.[3] If he were to decline the offer, he would lose his salary and, even worse, his position as an ordained minister. To be "let go" from his organization as a pastor would affect his reputation and result in all kinds of speculation as to the reason for the separation.

"God, is this really you?" Loren asked once again. He immediately felt a strong sense of God's peace and assurance that it was indeed his leading. Loren knew then what to do. He had to follow his heart and accept the consequences. He explained his position, and, as he expected, the head of the ministerial organization was unwilling to compromise on his position. After some discussion, they agreed that it would be best to separate amicably.

Walking away, Loren felt quite shaken and confused about what had just happened. This was a major contradiction to the outcome he had expected, making it a deep loss that pierced his heart.

As he was still figuring out what to do from this point, he was unaware that he was already moving toward the next challenge, which would turn out to be the most difficult experience of his life.

Loren went back to the motel room where they were staying and broke the news to his wife Darlene. They packed their belongings and headed home to California in their Volkswagen van.

Losing everything

They made the long trip, driving day and night. They drove overnight through the Arizona desert, and at around 6 a.m. Loren handed the wheel over to Darlene. He crawled into the back and climbed into a sleeping bag, where he closed his eyes, still pondering everything that had happened. First, he had given up his chance of a bright financial future in the family business. Now he had laid down the prospect of a successful career in the church. In following God's call to pioneer an international mission, he felt that he had given up everything. There was nothing left to give up. Now it was just him and Darlene.

Suddenly he was startled from his sleep and found himself being thrown around violently inside the van. With a sickening crunch of metal and glass, the vehicle was rolling – from its side to its top, to its other side, over and over down the highway. His head and body slammed against the inside walls. The van rolled over three times, and everything went black.

Loren regained consciousness and found himself lying on the roadside, with clouds of dust settling around him. He sat up in a daze. Nothing looked familiar. He was surrounded by Arizona desert, without a living soul in sight. Something warm and wet began to run down his head. He reached up to wipe it away, and his fingers came down covered with blood. His head ached, and he couldn't make sense of anything. Scattered around him was everything they owned: suitcases broken open, with shirts, underwear, and socks strewn around on the dirt.

He tried to remember what had happened – the difficult meeting, driving through the night, changing places with Darlene. Suddenly he froze. Where was Darlene? His eyes frantically searched the wreckage. Finally he saw her, lying face down under a heavy suitcase, a few yards away. He struggled to his knees and crawled to her. Lifting the suitcase, he saw a large gash on the back of her head. He turned her over and discovered that she was not breathing. Her eyes were wide open, but not seeing. Cold. Fixed. A shiver went through his whole body. Tears ran down his cheeks as he rocked her bloody head in his lap and tried to comprehend what had just happened. She was gone![4]

Total surrender

When Loren and I sat down for the interview, he recounted the experience.

"Those were the longest and darkest moments of my life," he recalled. "I felt totally alone, totally helpless – there was nothing I could do except hold her. I was crying and felt so hopeless – as never before and never since. It was truly the bleakest moment of my life, thinking I had lost what was dearest to my heart – Darlene."

Hopelessness and despair settled in as he looked around at the wreckage. It seemed to symbolize his life. Everything was gone.

"In that situation, God spoke to me," Loren described. "That was the only way I could make it through. There was not a living soul around me for miles, but I clearly heard a voice speaking my name. I looked around and I knew it must be God. I had never heard his voice audibly – but this time it was so loud and clear," Loren remembered. "He called my name and said, 'Loren, do you still want to serve me?' I wondered why he had to ask me that question, but I replied, 'God, I don't have anything left.' When I told him that he could have my life, he said, 'Pray for Darlene.' Up till then it hadn't even occurred to me to pray for her, because I thought she was dead. In that moment hopelessness turned to hope, and then hope turned to faith, because faith cometh by hearing – and hearing by the Word of God. So I followed what the Lord had said. I prayed as intensely and loudly as I could, and as I prayed, Darlene's eyes shut and she began to breathe."

What he didn't know was that at exactly that time, 11:20 a.m., God had told twelve ladies in a prayer meeting in Los Angeles to pray for Darlene and him, and they did. In San Francisco, another woman had also responded to the Lord's voice and was praying for them.

"I don't know if there were others, but this was an amazing miracle for me that allowed me to get through this horrific experience. My back was hurt and I had all kinds of other injuries – but when I heard God's voice I knew the Lord's presence, and that was the most important thing to me," Loren shares.

Just a short time after Darlene began to breathe, other things started to happen. A passing driver went for help, and half an hour later they were in the ambulance on their way to the hospital. It took several days before Darlene was released from the hospital, but Loren left the same day – shoeless and walking stiffly in bloodstained clothes. His shoes and other possessions were still waiting beside the wrecked van.

"What was burned into my heart that day was a lesson on the power that God can release when we lay down our rights," he explained. "I thought I'd lost everything. I never realized that nothing in this life actually belongs to me. I would speak of *my* car, *my* wife, *my* ministry. After the accident, I realized for the first time how easily I could lose it all in seconds."

Loren described his realization to me. "Everything we have is just given to us for a time to use for God's glory. These new thoughts started me on a quest through Scripture to learn what God had to say on the important subject."

The X Factors

"Out of this experience the Lord showed me that relinquishing rights is actually the key to the rewards where God releases blessing and brings forth new ministries," Loren said. "With every ministry birthed, you always go through 'the cross' – through a process where unclean motives, attitudes and actions die," he continued to explain. "For each ministry that is birthed, somebody has to pay a price for it to start, whether it's reaching out to the homeless or gangs or teenagers, or whether it's our mercy ships taking doctors and medical teams into areas that are unreachable by plane."

Loren believes that every great vision must go through specific stages in order to have a lasting impact and collaborate with God's great calling. He calls those stages *The Five Xs*.

The first X stands for **excitement over the vision**. The Gospel of Luke illustrates this in chapter 5, where Jesus called his first disciples: Peter, James, and John. Jesus borrowed Peter's boat to preach to the crowd from the shore. Then Jesus turned to Peter and told him to take the boat out on the sea and cast his net again. They had caught nothing all night, but Peter followed Jesus' instructions and went out again. And this time they caught multitudes of fish.

"The disciples were amazed and excited about this miracle, but even greater excitement came when Jesus expanded their vision and told them, 'You will be fishers of men,'" Loren explained. This went far beyond what they could imagine for their lives. "In other words, Jesus told them that there would be a great release of people who would come to know Christ." On hearing that initial vision, there was great excitement among the disciples, and they left everything and followed Jesus. Loren explains that with every great vision, the first stage is excitement.

The second X refers to **the experimental phase**. This is illustrated in Luke 10. Jesus sent out seventy of his disciples with instructions to cure the sick, cast out demons, and preach the good news of the kingdom in his name. He told them that he was sending them out like lambs in the midst of wolves, and gave them a specific set of instructions for this outreach. "They came back rejoicing and said, 'Lord, in your name even the demons submit to us!'" The seventy disciples experienced the reality of Jesus' power working through them as they stepped out; thus, their faith experiment succeeded.

"But the experimental phase is followed by **an exam**, the third X," Loren pointed out. "The exam phase has all to do with exposing the motives of the disciples' hearts." This is demonstrated in John 6:28, where some of Jesus' followers asked him, "What shall we do, that we may work the works of God?" This time, instead of giving them a formula, Jesus replied, "This is the work of God, that you believe in Him whom He sent."

In the passage, Jesus continued to explain that they must "eat the flesh of the Son of Man and drink His blood" (John 6:53). In other words, he told them to depend on him, to partake of his nature, and to take in his life. The key to accessing the kingdom of God is relationship, not formula, and many of the disciples could not understand this mystery. Instead, they kept asking Jesus to perform a sign so that they would believe. And when Jesus did not give them what they wanted, many were offended. At that point many turned away and followed him no longer. They wanted a method, not the mystery of the cross. They wanted power, not dependency on Christ. "The cross of Christ examines our deepest motives," Loren pinpointed in our conversation. "Our heart is purged and purified, and we go through things we don't want to go through. The cross is not something that you 'gladly bear', even though an old hymn puts it that way. But we go through the experience of the cross to let our selfish ways die, because we know we will come out purified on the other side."

The same can be seen in the example of Peter. "When Peter was faced with the reality of the cross, he denied Jesus. But his heart was purged through this experience," Loren continued. At this point, Peter moved into **the executive stage** – the fourth X. "After Peter repented and was restored, he had the authority to stand before multitudes and declare Jesus as Lord," Loren explained. The Peter who had denied Jesus was not the same Peter who stood before the multitudes on the day of Pentecost in Acts 2. On that day, when the crowd accused the disciples of being drunk, he stood up and preached Jesus without fear of man. He had undergone a powerful transformation process that had purged him of his insecurities and self-reliance. Now he could move into the fullness of God's calling on his life.

The last X, according to Loren, is **exponential growth**. It is illustrated in the same account about the day of Pentecost. After Peter preached with passion before the crowd, 3,000 believers were added to their number (Acts 2:41).

Loren affirmed that he sees people and ministries moving through these five phases all the time. "When people begin to be more spiritually entrepreneurial, they create new ministries with God. But they all go through these stages before they experience exponential growth."

Loren has definitely walked through this process himself in pioneering and leading Youth With A Mission. Having gone through the first four stages, the ministry is experiencing exponential growth to this day. Since 1960, YWAM has grown rapidly, and with the participation of more than five million short-term volunteers and 20,000 long-term staff, YWAM now operates in more than 1,100 locations in 191 countries in the world, and sends five ships with medical teams and provisions into the poorest and furthest nations that are not reachable by plane.

In 1977 Loren founded a training centre in Kona, Hawaii, which has developed into the University of the Nations (UofN), a modular university operating in 142 countries. It offers courses in medical care, media, arts and entertainment, economics, cross-cultural missions, and of course biblical studies. Loren says, "We train people to bring transformation. To us, missions is a lot broader than a person wearing a pith-helmet under a shady tree talking to a non-white. Missions for us is knowing God and making him known in every sphere of society – and that's what we are training for."

Knowing God

Loren has seen his vision come true. Young people are becoming leaders and transforming society. And this is the result of one man's obedience to God's voice – his dedication to the vision, to the call and destiny on his life. It has had a ripple effect, launching thousands into their own destiny and changing millions of lives. As the revivalist Henry Varley once said to the great evangelist D. L. Moody, "The world has yet to see what God can do with a man that is totally surrendered to him."[5] We can see a glimpse of that in Loren Cunningham and the story of Youth With A Mission.

Despite the ministry's exponential growth, Loren continues to operate in the background. Even though he has talked to some of the highest government officials and world leaders, and is friends with kings and queens, he has not allowed his face to be the symbol of YWAM. "It's not about my face; I want young people to be released and take the leadership," Loren explains. "And that is what our heart is: we want to see people released to fulfil the great commission instead of controlling them." What he says is true.

Loren's remarkable humility can be traced back to his testing in the desert, where he held his seemingly lifeless wife in his arms and relinquished his rights to God. God has released abundant blessings on his life, but those blessings, according to Loren, are not the point. Instead, his focus is on his deep friendship with God and the knowledge of his nearness. That is his place of rest, joy, and abundance – not the circumstances in his life.

"Since that time of intense testing, nothing is more important to me than the nearness of God. It is so important because God is the God of all comfort and he wants to give us comfort in those times when we are overwhelmed and facing difficult circumstances," Loren explains. "You learn more about him in suffering than you do in the good times! In the horrific circumstance when I picked up my wife for dead in the desert, I experienced the nearness of the Lord – the valley where it seemed most hopeless and I felt most lonely. After that experience, I felt an overwhelming sense of his nearness, which has never left me, and I have learned to rest in it."

Even though he still faces many challenges and stresses, Loren has learned to keep himself in check and in faith, resting in God's provision. "Hebrews talks about the rest of faith. I am living a life of faith, because faith cometh by hearing. I listen daily to the Lord and practice his presence. I've heard what I am to do, and I expect God to show up. To me this is the key: to hear and obey. It's simple, and we should not make it complicated."

Loren Cunningham is probably the only person on earth who has literally preached the gospel to *every nation on earth*. Yet even now, at eighty-two years of age, he is far from ready to retire and sit back! Loren has heard the call of God to reach out to the 1,776 Bibleless languages that still exist worldwide and end their "Bible poverty" (the lack of a Bible in their language). To achieve this, his mission is to deliver the New Testament in an oral recording in each of those languages by 2020. A full 426 of these languages can be found in the Pacific island region, 321 of which are in the remote islands surrounding Indonesia, the Philippines, and Papua New Guinea. This region is where YWAM is currently putting its emphasis.

Humanly speaking, this task seems impossible, but with God all things are possible.[6] And when you hear God speak, you can trust that he will make a way, and that his commission is always a Mission Possible.

Chapter Five
Enduring Faith

Facing loss and disappointment

Bill Johnson

> Most of what you need in life will come to you, but
> most of what you want you'll need to go and get. For
> you to come into your destiny will not be brought to
> you on a silver platter. There is a fight that must be
> gone through: one of persistence, one of diligence, one
> of knowing how to face loss and how to bring strength
> and courage to yourself in the midst of confusion.
>
> *Bill Johnson*

It was August 2003. Bill Johnson and Randy Clark were ministering at a healing conference in Brazil. People's lives were being transformed, the presence of God was tangible, and testimonies of incredible healings were multiplying each day. Just the night before, several tumours had disappeared from people's bodies, and expectant hope for God's presence to invade human circumstances had turned to exhilarating faith.

The phone rang as Bill and Randy were reviewing the testimonies from the day before. Bill could see it was from home.

"I'd better pick this up," he said.

"How did Dad's surgery go?" Bill asked his wife, Beni. His dad had been scheduled for a minor gall bladder operation, and even though it was just a routine procedure, Bill was eager to receive an update and hear that everything had gone well. He had always considered his family to be the greatest treasure in his life, and guarded it with tremendous gratitude and care.

What he heard next, however, would thrust him into one of the most trying seasons in his life. It confronted him with questions and a major contradiction. It would test and try by fire what he believed about God, his calling, and the vision in his heart.

"They found *cancer*?" Bill said in disbelief.

"Yes, pancreatic cancer," Beni replied. "The prognosis does not look good. They don't give him much time."

Bill tried to process what he had just heard. Fuelled by the miracles he had seen over the previous days, he replied, "We won't bow down to this. This can't stay. This is not the work of God, and we will contend for healing as we always do."

Just a few months before, Bill had taken on the assignment to contend for a cancer-free zone at Bethel Church and the surrounding region in northern California. This had not been an act of presumption, but of deep conviction from Scripture that God is good and that his goodness expresses itself in healing. He is the same yesterday, today, and forever, and the fact that he is the healer does not change. This conviction had become a foundational cornerstone of Bill's faith in the preceding years, and he saw God work in wonderful ways, as more and more people were healed from incurable and terminal diseases. And, more significantly, it was his father who had taught him these truths and laid the foundation for the move of God that Bethel was experiencing.

Upon hearing the news of his dad's diagnosis, Bill immediately flew back home to be with his family. Then he did what he knew to do: he prayed, contended for healing, worshipped, and ministered to his dad, along with many other believers across the nation.

In our interview, Bill explained, "My father was known for his wisdom, stature, and character. He released many young men and women into ministry that nobody else would believe in. He just gave them favour when seemingly no one else would because they were different. So numerous people joined us in contending for a breakthrough for my dad."

Holding the course

Several people warned Bill not to get his hopes up too high. They cautioned him to be realistic in view of the prognosis – but Bill would not budge in his conviction about pursuing the full manifestation of God's promise of healing.

Praying for his father day and night, Bill applied every principle for healing that he knew. However, in spite of all of those prayers, Earl Johnson's body began to deteriorate. Soon he began to look gaunt and unhealthy, as the physical signs of cancer eating up his body became more pronounced each day. Within only a short period of time, Earl Johnson looked to have aged about twenty years. His body had turned to skin and bones.

In the midst of all of this physical transformation, Earl would not let himself be distracted by outward appearances. "We all noticed that he would refuse to look into the mirror or pay attention to the decay of his body. Even when he walked to the restroom and washed his hands, he would not look up from the sink into the mirror. He was determined not to look at the problem, but to keep his focus on God's promises," Bill recalls.

But the boulder of cancer would not budge, no matter how hard they pushed with prayer, fasting, and worship. Bill and his family and friends had seen so many people healed of cancer, yet right in their midst the sickness would not bow. It was an exhausting, fierce, and hellish battle. And in the end, to all outward appearances, they lost: four months after Earl Johnson's diagnosis, he passed away.

Dealing with disappointment

This was one of the greatest disappointments and losses Bill has ever had to face. "My dad was a wonderful leader. He had so much wisdom, so much experience, and he was a man of great stature," he explains. "But he was also my best friend, the greatest source of encouragement in my life. So there was the tremendous personal loss of a wonderful father, and the great ministry loss – and it was very important to process this loss in the right way."

Bill recognized the importance of dealing with the contradiction and seeming defeat in this battle against cancer. How would he resolve the conflict between his father's death from cancer and his firm belief in the healing power of God? How would he process the loss? How would he deal with the grief, the pain, and the disappointment?

"When unexpected things happen, there's always that sense of setback or disappointment, but I don't have to feed myself with that," Bill says. "There is always a choice to make. It's like having two plates of food. I don't have to eat rotten food. I can make a decision to feed myself with what God is doing instead of what he isn't doing. That has been a saving grace for us over the years when we've had to deal with major disappointments."

Bill admits there are a lot of things he cannot explain, and he does not try to do so. He leaves them in an area he calls "mystery". "What I do understand, at least in some measure, is God's goodness," Bill says. "I see what he is doing. I can eat off that plate. If I feed on disappointment, I will be offended at God, but I can't afford that. I cannot afford to slip into unbelief where I am unintentionally resisting what God is doing. If I start dwelling on things for which there is no answer, that's just inviting offence."

This is one reason why Bethel Church places such a high value on testimonies. Not a Sunday service goes by without a testimony being shared. And no day goes by without Bill seeking out a new testimony. "If I hear of anybody who has a story to tell, I grab a hold of them. I need to feed on what God is doing, because I know I'm weak. I'm just ten minutes away from depression if I allow myself to go down the spiral of focusing on problems and contradictions. I deliberately shut out negative voices and surround myself with stories about God's goodness to build my faith," he explains.

Two conflicting realities

A common misunderstanding among Christians when tragedy and crisis hit is this: that it must have been God's will. After all, the Scriptures do talk about suffering, so when sickness strikes, many believe it is part of the suffering we are called to (and thus must be ordained by God). Bill is convinced that this is a tragic misconception. "The reference to suffering in the Scriptures is an invitation to live in between two conflicting realities: the truth of God's promise and the contradiction of actual experience. Bearing the cross is not to be confused with suffering from sickness and disease. Instead, it means living in between these two conflicting realities, yet still trusting God," he explains.

Focusing on God's goodness is necessary to keep from losing sight of the truth that transcends present reality. However, it does not mean that we should push away the pain or ignore unanswered questions. It's important to grieve and mourn over a loss in the right way. For Bill, healthy mourning meant not demanding an answer to why his father had died and why they hadn't seen the breakthrough promised in God's Word.

Healthy mourning

"I am happy for God to give me clarity on anything, but I am not going to hold him hostage to an answer," Bill emphasizes. "We mourned together as a family. Mourning is very important, in measure. When it gets unhealthy, though, mourning can take you to unbelief."

In Mark 16, the disciples mourned the death of Jesus, and they were so locked into mourning that they didn't believe credible witnesses who said that Jesus had risen. They didn't believe the women who said he was raised from the dead. They didn't believe the disciples who had walked with him on the road to Emmaus (Luke 24). Their depth of mourning did not allow them to believe. "So mourning is healthy in measure, but if it causes you to start questioning God's nature, his covenant, and his promise, it leads you down a dead-end road. I can't afford to do that. It's too deep a hole to fall into, and it's too hard to crawl out," Bill says.

It's important to note that the process of grieving may look different for every individual. There is no standard recipe. However, it is crucial to not seek answers where there is no answer. *Pain doesn't need an answer; pain needs a touch of God.* So I'm just there, and I weep with those who weep," Bill explains.

Bill processed the loss together with his family, but he also went through a personal process of mourning. "The best way for me to mourn is with God. I get before God and am really honest – but I will never accuse him. I say, 'God, this hurts so much. I really thought things would turn out differently. It feels like you broke your promise. I know it's not possible, because that violates who you are. I understand that. But that's what it feels like. That's why I need you to heal me. I need you to touch me. I am not asking for explanations. If you were to give me understanding, I would love it, because I love to understand things. But I don't need it to trust you.' That's my process."

Principles to victory

The first thing Bill does when facing disappointment and contradictions is to turn to the Word of God. "That's my automatic response," Bill shares. "I get into the Word, especially when I am in pain. I usually go to the Psalms and read until I hear my own voice in them. When I hear the cry of my heart in a psalm, then I know I've found a home, and I stay there. I pray it, I sing it, I meditate on it, I feed my soul on it."

This, however, is a process, and it does not happen instantly. "I've had situations in my life where God would touch me and speak to me, but an hour later I would be troubled again. I would go back and read until he talked to me again, and an hour later I would do the same again, and an hour later again – until finally it becomes so much a part of you that you're able to live from what he has fed you," Bill explains.

Sometimes, though, the pain speaks so loudly, the soul is so troubled, and the heart so restless that it can be difficult to quiet yourself and hear God's voice. In those situations, you have to keep pressing in to find that place of peace. "Sometimes it's hard," Bill admits. "But I also know through experience that there's life when I hear his voice – and I want that more than I want all the other voices. If it is hard for me to read, I may read out loud. I may walk around the room and read."

For Bill, sometimes even reading is not enough. He continues, "If I have been reading for half an hour and I don't remember a thing I've read because I am so distracted, I just take a break and begin to worship." Worship takes Bill to yet another level, but not just any worship. "I specifically worship him in areas that seem to be contradictory to what I am experiencing. If I have no money and I need money, I'll honour him for being generous, for being the provider. If somebody has died that we prayed for to be healed, I will exalt him for being the healer. I go contrary to what's worrying me and warring in my mind until I get a breakthrough in experiencing the presence of God."

This level of processing is not always comfortable or low key. Bill explains, "I will only get that breakthrough if I go beyond what is convenient. I can't just sit there and be quiet and timid. I will give a sacrifice of worship and demonstrate it. Sometimes I'll dance; sometimes I'll shout. I have to go outside what feels comfortable. Once I do that, the heaviness breaks and the Word begins to open up to me."

In processing grief and pain, it is important to stay proactive and not passive. Bill was very intentional in how he faced the death of his father. "As soon as my dad died, I went out and prayed for someone who had cancer," Bill explains. "If you are moving forward, it's easier to focus. If you are idle or passive, pain and loss will take over and fill your mind. I would make a special effort to serve people and give my heart direction instead of letting pain and conflict take over."

He continues, "I want to hear God's voice about my life, not just about the loss of my dad. I only have a certain number of days on the earth and I want to be found faithful. I want to do what he made possible for me to do, and so I search the Word until I hear him speak to me, because I need it. I don't just sit back with an empty mind doing nothing. I won't let my mind be idle to entertain wrong things, because then I'm in trouble."

Being authentic

As the senior pastor of a world-impacting church, and as an international speaker, Bill feels a pressure to appear strong for the people he leads and influences. But he refuses to give in to that pressure and appear to be something he is not. What ultimately makes him a person of such greatness and stature is his transparency and authenticity. What you see is what you get. When he weeps, he weeps. And when he rejoices, he rejoices. He never tries to pretend to have answers when he does not. He never tries to appear strong when he is not. This willingness to reveal weakness is exactly what makes him a strong person.

The challenge for every leader is to juggle personal tragedy, pain, and weakness with standing strong in public ministry.

More often than not, the two don't seem to go together. Not so with Bill. He has made a deliberate choice to be the same person at church or on the platform as he is at home. Throughout his personal battle with grief over his father's death, he let the whole church journey with him as a family. He never pretended to be anything he wasn't. Bill describes this process: "I didn't come to the church with canned answers or formulas. I just let them watch us while we processed our grief, and I tried to be honest. This is what I have committed my life to, and it doesn't change when there is tragic loss."

Still, while Bill is transparent with his emotions, he does not let the pain rule him. "I can't let that happen," he says. "I have been in that hole before and it's too hard to escape from. I don't want to go there again, and I don't believe it's necessary."

A unique offering

Bill sees pain and disappointment as an opportunity to give God a unique kind of offering. In his pain, he comes before God and tells him how he feels. He tells God that he is disappointed, confused, and hurting. He shares the emotions from his heart, and then offers God his praise. "This is my offering, because I know that in heaven I won't have any sorrow, I won't have any pain, and I won't be confused," he says. "So I say to God, 'I'm going to give you a gift *now* that I won't have the chance to give you there.'"

He continues, "I believe worshipping God in the midst of pain is the most unique kind of offering you can give. The pain is the flavour in the offering, and it is precious to God because it is costly. This is what my dad taught us to do: in all things give praise. So we celebrate God's goodness in the midst of disappointment and loss, because we know he is good, and we know he didn't cause or orchestrate this tragedy. I don't understand it, but I know he will make it work for good."

The voice of accusation

Accusation always waits at the door of pain and disappointment. This can take the form of accusing God and taking offence. Or it can lead to guilt and shame. The voice of accusation is always looking for an opportune time to creep in and is no respecter of persons. Bill has fought this battle, and it is common to all Christians when they experience a crisis. The most challenging voice Bill dealt with was one of self-doubt: Is there anything I could have done differently? Was there anything I did wrong?

Bill explains how he handles that voice: "There is still the reality that everyone Jesus ministered to received healing. That's the standard. Not everyone I minister to gets healed, and when it's the one who matters to me the most, that's a devastating loss. But I also know if I take the blame, there is no redemptive purpose for me. I can't afford to do guilt and shame. If it worked, I would do it, but it doesn't work. I've been there many times. It just takes me deeper into the hole of mistrusting God and myself, and it's a horrible trap. So I can't accuse God, but I also can't go down the road of accusing myself."

Bill instead calls on God. He explains, "I need help, because it looks like maybe I should have fasted or prayed more or done something else. That's where I say to God, 'I need you to talk to me; your voice heals me. If you'll speak to me I'll know I am okay.'"

Bill clarifies that God doesn't have to talk to him about what is actually hurting him: "All he needs to do is just speak to me. I may be hurting over this loss, and he talks to me about a completely different subject. If he is talking, there's healing in his voice, so I look for his voice and his presence."

Adjusting the way you hear

Many people have experienced a dry season in their lives where they have found it difficult to hear God's voice. Bill is no exception. For him, these seasons when God seems silent usually correspond with situations that are really challenging and tough – those times when we desperately need to hear from God.

"I have had times when it was hard for me to hear God's voice, but usually it was because of anxiety. My own anxiety made it hard to hear," Bill explains. "It was not God who did not want to speak to me. God is the Word – it's hard for him not to have anything to say." What Bill discovered again and again after those times when God seemed silent was that God had only changed the way he spoke, and Bill hadn't recognized his voice. He realized that he had to adjust the way he listened.

Bill goes on, "For example, Moses saw a burning bush. That's a very unusual circumstance, but it was God. Sometimes you have an unusual circumstance in your life, and it's actually the Lord asking for your attention. The Bible says when Moses turned *aside*, the Lord spoke to him. I remember years ago we had some unusual circumstances, and finally we turned aside, and then God spoke. *Sometimes we do not hear him because we do not recognize his voice. We need to adjust our hearing, because he might speak in a different way from what we are used to.*"

Bill conquers feelings of guilt, shame, and accusation by hearing God's voice, whether through the Word, prayer, worship, or simply turning aside to listen. There is comfort in his voice, and it calms the storm of confusion, turmoil, and pain. The voice settles the truth in your heart and releases a peace that goes beyond understanding (see Philippians 4:7).

Enduring faith

Just a few days before Earl Johnson died, Bill preached a powerful message on upholding truth in the midst of contradictory experiences. Four months earlier, God had given him an assignment to push against what he called the "boulder of cancer". And so he had pushed against this huge boulder day and night, from every angle, with every principle he'd ever learned about healing.

He described his battle: "I've pushed it high, I've pushed it low, I've stood against it, and I've run against it. I've done everything I know to do, but the rock has not budged – yet." Bill went on to say that he would not sacrifice what he knew to be true, no matter what happened with his father's cancer. He declared that he would not budge from God's truth, regardless of circumstances.

He continued in the sermon, "You can't push against something like that day after day, week after week, month after month, without building a strength you didn't know you had. There is a 500-pound boulder that four months ago I couldn't have pushed, but today is being threatened by what I can push – *if* I will not allow my heart to get spoiled and embittered and offended at God! If I will keep my heart clean, the strength that I have built in this push *will* pay off. It's impossible for it not to pay off."

Five days after Bill preached that sermon, Earl Johnson passed away. He went out like a champion, but, to all outward appearances, his death looked like a defeat. Yet a few months later, the tables turned. At the time, Bill was in the middle of writing his book *Strengthening Yourself in the Lord*. He gave it to a staff member to read, and this person told him, "I really enjoyed it, but I wondered why you didn't share the story of your dad and your loss, because as a whole church we learned by watching you process that grief."

Taking that advice to heart, Bill went back and added a chapter about his father's cancer battle. One thing he added was that the Lord had given him a word from Proverbs 6, which says that when somebody steals something from another person, they have to pay it back seven times (Proverbs 6:31). Based on that word, Bill believed in God for a seven-times greater anointing for the healing of cancer than before.

The day Bill completed the additional chapter on his dad's cancer battle, including his interpretation of the word in Proverbs 6, he left his office and went straight to a prayer meeting. As soon as he walked in, a lady walked up to him and asked, "Do you remember me?"

"No, I don't," Bill replied.

"A few weeks ago, you prayed for me! I had pancreatic cancer, and I've been healed!"

There it was: pancreatic cancer. Her healing demonstrated God's redemptive justice. From that time on, God continued to deliver increase and breakthrough. The enemy's victory is never permanent. Never. And that was GOD'S AMEN.

Bill, his family, and the whole Bethel Community never allowed their hearts to be discouraged by contradictory experiences. Instead, they kept their faith in the goodness and healing power of God. They have since seen the Lord honour their perseverance and heal countless people of all kinds of sicknesses and diseases, particularly cancer.

They have learned to stand strong in the midst of trials and testing, knowing that the outcome of their faith produces strength and maturity, which glorifies God in a unique way (James 1:3–4). As Bill puts it, faith brings answers, but *enduring* faith brings answers with character. This is what he lives, this is what he teaches, and this is what the Bethel community is living. It demonstrates how a community of believers that shows the fruits of the Spirit and moves in the power of the Spirit opens the door for God's kingdom to come and for heaven to invade earth!

Chapter Six
Against All Odds

Breaking through fear and rejection

Dr Sandra Kennedy

It always seems impossible until it's done.
Nelson Mandela

Imagine you are a therapist who has been treating clients who have so-called "visions" – and then you have one yourself!

Dr Sandra Kennedy was driving home along the interstate outside Dallas, Texas, when she suddenly felt a presence in her car and completely lost touch with her surroundings. In that moment, she was caught up in a vision in which she found herself standing in a plaza, looking at a plate-glass building. She looked to her right, and Jesus himself was standing next to her. He explained that the building before her was a church – the church that she was going to start and pastor.

He said, "Its name is Whole Life Ministries, and here you will grow up the body of Christ and teach them victory."

Then Jesus walked her through the building, showing her the sanctuary, the healing centre, the freedom centre, the offices, the academy, the café, and the bookshop. Sandra absorbed the exact size, layout, colours, departments, and interior design, down to the last detail.

Jesus spoke as they walked: "People will be set free by my Spirit and stay free by my Word." He gave her more and more details: from how to set up the church board to how to run the church on a daily basis. He gave her every single aspect of the church's operation. He also revealed that the church was to be in Augusta, Georgia – and, by the way, it was going to be racially mixed: half black and half white. In Augusta, Georgia – the South. In the 1970s. Where they were having racial riots!

In an instant, she found herself driving in her car again. Her heart was pounding, her body shaking, her face pale. Thousands of thoughts raced through her mind as she tried to gather herself. "What on earth was that? This is insane!" she thought. "Or even worse, I'm insane!" After all, from her work as a therapist she knew a whole lot about people who had *visions*... "I'm worse than all of my clients put together!" she exclaimed.

She had no idea who had been driving while she had been having this vision, or how she had got to where she was now. How was it possible that the car was still safely on the interstate, still driving in the direction of home? It was crazy. But the vision itself was even more crazy. Everything about it was far-fetched. For one thing, at that time she had never heard of a woman starting, let alone pastoring, a church! Especially from her perspective as a born-and-bred Southern Baptist. They didn't believe in women preachers – and neither did she.

In addition, of course, the idea of a racially mixed congregation in the American South also seemed ludicrous in the 1970s. She could find very little in the vision that made any sense. Except for one thing, which didn't let her go: the promise that God would use her in healing.

At that time, Baptists didn't believe in supernatural healing, either. But healing was something Sandra had believed in from early childhood, when she had had her first encounter with God.

Sandra was about nine years old, living with her mother, older brother, and younger sister on her stepfather's farm. One day, as she played outside, she heard a voice – whether it was audible or internal, she doesn't know. But it was so loud and clear to her that she turned around to look for the person speaking. It said, "One day I will use you in healing ministry!"

Instantly, Sandra knew it was God and took the words to heart. It made such a deep impression on her that, with childlike faith, she started to pray for every sick animal on the farm – even the dead rats! She also preached to everything that was alive and moving. In her childlike mind, she reasoned that if God was God, then he was God – and he must be greater than all earthly limitations. He had to be the healer and deliverer, and he had to be able to set people free. Why else should she believe in him and serve him?

No animal was ever healed or raised from the dead during that period of her life, but the encounter with God started a process in her heart. From then on, she believed in the reality of God's ability to heal – and that he intended to use her somehow to do it. This belief would go on to release miracles later in her life.

However, Sandra never witnessed a healing or a miracle until she was in her mid-twenties, when she visited a charismatic church for the first time. She was working for the Southern Baptist denomination at their headquarters. One day, her boss there emphatically warned her not to go to a certain Baptist church, because they were holding "strange" charismatic meetings. This warning, however, was enough to make her want to go and check it out...

Her heart was on guard but her mind was curious when she entered the church. She immediately felt a special presence, an atmosphere as if people were expecting something to happen. She also felt her heart being warmed and surrounded by love. Then, during the service, several people with various back injuries received prayer, and Sandra saw them being healed. It made a deep impression on her.

But there was something else that impressed her too. The people there seemed to be very genuine. They were clearly living changed lives. Sandra felt convicted, because she knew her spiritual life was not what it was supposed to be. This was even though she had attended seminary, had worked as a youth director in a 3,000-member church, and was now on staff at Southern Baptist headquarters. She found herself one day following God and the next day following the world, doing things she knew she shouldn't be doing. She was full of compromise. When Sandra saw how the lives of these people had been transformed, it stirred everything within her to seek God for a real transformation.

She continued to attend that church. One night, after another meeting, she went home and had a very vivid dream involving an angel showing her the dire condition of her spiritual walk. She woke up horrified, not sure if she was right with God. So she began to pray. After praying all night and throughout the next day, in one moment she suddenly felt Jesus' presence with her in her room, and the power of God came over her. This encounter transformed her heart in an instant. She would never be the same. The following night she had a similar vivid dream, only this time the angel in the dream confirmed that she was right with God.

The heavenly typewriter

Stirred by the healings she saw in those church meetings, Sandra prayed for several months for more understanding and insight on healing. Then one day she received a phone call from her brother. "You need to come home. Mother is dying. She is in a semi-coma and has less than forty-eight hours to live," he said. Sandra's mother was already being treated for cancer, but this sudden deterioration took everyone by surprise. Sandra immediately booked the next flight home.

As she sat in her seat on the aeroplane, Sandra prayed that she would make it home in time. Then she heard something that sounded like a typewriter. And with the rhythm of the keystrokes, she heard these words being spoken: "Our Father which art in heaven, hallowed be thy name. Thy kingdom come, thy will be done, on earth as it is in heaven. *Tell your mother there is no sickness in heaven!*" Sandra looked all around, but could not discern anyone who had been talking to her, nor did she see a typewriter.

She found herself feeling scared half to death. "What on earth was that?" she wondered. She didn't know what to make of it. She was even more frightened when she heard the same message and the sound of a typewriter a second time. Was she making this up? When she heard it a third time, loud and clear, it dawned on her that God might be speaking to her. But then she immediately began arguing with God. "How am I going to tell her this? My mother is a Baptist! She knows that's not even all of the Lord's Prayer. God, I need you to tell this to someone else as well as me!"

When Sandra arrived at her mother's farmhouse, she received a call from her sister. What her sister said next was familiar: "I need to tell you something! I had this strange dream last night. I heard a voice say, 'Our Father which art in heaven, hallowed be thy name. Thy kingdom come, thy will be done, on earth as it is in heaven. Tell your mother there is no sickness in heaven!' Do you know what this means?"

Stunned, Sandra replied, "I'm not sure. But God told me the very same words, so I guess we had better follow his instructions."

Still not quite sure what to do, the family gathered by their mother's bed. And they simply began to declare the exact words that they had heard – the first part of the Lord's Prayer, followed by the promise that there is no sickness in heaven. For five hours, they did nothing else but speak these words over their mother.

Nothing seemed to happen for a while, but as they continued to make the declaration their mother's eyes started moving. She seemed to be waking up from the semi-coma. Sandra got excited and prayed even more boldly. Suddenly, the thought came to her mind that she should anoint her mother with oil.

Crisco anointing

Sandra had never seen anybody being anointed with oil. It was not a common practice among most Christians back then. But she ran anyway to search the kitchen for oil. Once there, all she could find was a can of Crisco (lard). And since it was the closest thing to oil that was available, she decided it would have to do. Sandra and her sister dragged their mother into the kitchen and sat her in a chair.

Now there was another problem. Where did you put the "oil"? Sandra knew that the Bible said something somewhere about anointing the sick with oil, but she did not know exactly where, and she didn't have time to look it up to find out exactly how to do it. Without any real clue, she followed her intuition and started spreading Crisco on her mother's forehead. Since it didn't seem to be doing any harm, she continued along her mother's face, then her head, her hair, her shoulders... Before they knew it, they had greased their mother from head to toe with Crisco, including the chair she was sitting on! (Please don't follow this example as a prototype for praying for the sick!)

Everything looked pretty ridiculous. But at the very moment when Sandra used up the last of the Crisco, her mother woke up completely and started speaking fluently. But to the daughters' surprise, the first thing she did was express her concern about what they'd been praying! "What if this sickness is of the Lord, and I am supposed to die?" she asked.

Sandra was taken aback by this. "Then why are you taking all this medicine? If this illness is of the Lord, you don't want to go against the Lord by doing that, either!" she exclaimed sarcastically.

Her mother continued to argue against prayer for healing, so Sandra gathered up all of her medication and threw it in the trash. "Then she really woke up!" Sandra laughed as she described the scene in our interview.

Eventually, her mother began to realize how inconsistent her view of God was with Scripture. When she repented for believing that the sickness was from God, the power of God came over her, and she was completely healed in an instant.

They were all amazed, shocked, and excited. What a miracle, and what a breakthrough!

That night, Sandra learned how rewarding it is to simply listen to God's voice and follow his instructions – even though it looked silly, even though she didn't understand it all and didn't know how to do it "properly". But she took a leap of faith – and what an amazing answer they witnessed. The medical records for her mother later confirmed the healing with one word: "Miracle".

Burying the vision

Now, driving down the interstate, Sandra seemed to be hearing from God again. And even though she had heard God speak to her several times before, she still found herself scared to death by this vision. From her work counselling patients, she had spoken with a whole lot of people who'd had so-called *visions* – and now she'd just had one herself! It scared the wits out of her. Who would she be able to tell?

"After all, I'm a therapist," Sandra reasoned. "I'd better keep my mouth shut and pretend this never happened."

But forgetting about the incident was easier said than done. When she arrived home safe and sound, she continued to feel unsettled and confused; in fact, her whole life felt as if it had been turned upside down.

In an attempt to bury the confusion about this visitation at the back of her mind, for the next seven years Sandra threw herself into her job and kept herself busy with a sixty-hour work week. This seemed to help her forget for a while, but her busy life and routine were shaken up again when she experienced exactly the same vision a second time – this time during a Christian conference in Florida. Again, she found herself in the same plaza before the same plate-glass building. Again, Jesus showed her around the entire building and gave her specific instructions.

This time, Sandra thought she probably needed to share the vision with someone. So she shared it with one friend, who believed in her and didn't think she was crazy. This response encouraged Sandra to talk to other ministers. Unfortunately, none of them understood what she was talking about, and neither did they believe she should or could pursue the vision.

"I was quite insecure and wanted the approval of the people I knew and valued," Sandra explains. "That was my pitfall. I wanted to hear from people that I could do this, that I was not crazy. The vision and calling to pastor a church was just beyond anything I could comprehend. I went to all my friends who were pastors, and everybody told me that this was crazy, that I couldn't do this. I was intimidated by these voices and so I didn't dare to pursue it."

Divine pursuit

Sandra was limited by her insecurity and fear of what people would think. "It was a time when women were not permitted to preach, let alone pastor a church," Sandra says. "Even today it's hard, but back then in the seventies it was unthinkable. I was looking for man to pat me on the shoulder and say it was okay for me to do this," she explains. "A crucial lesson for me was that I had to learn to be myself instead of trying to be superwoman and gain everybody's approval. I had tried to meet everyone's expectations and please everyone – that's why

I was stuck for so long. I had to get settled in who I was and what I was called to do."

That lesson took Sandra eleven years to learn. After the negative response to her vision from others, she again turned to throwing herself into her career. And she was outwardly successful, which confirmed in her mind that she was doing the right thing. She describes that time period: "Good is the enemy of best – and I had this really good job offer which seemed the best to me. I made good money and got to work with major leaders in the therapy field. So I settled for that." Another eleven years passed.

Overcoming insecurity

In those years before venturing into her life call, God was working on Sandra. One obstacle that she had to overcome was insecurity, which was rooted in wrong beliefs about God and about herself.

"I struggled a lot with shame, guilt, and condemnation. I had not been living as a saint for a great part of my life. Even though I had considered myself a Christian, I was full of compromise. I struggled with feelings of not being good enough, smart enough, qualified enough – you name it," Sandra explains. She simply could not see herself as a good candidate for the job described in the vision, so it was beyond her comprehension.

She describes the battle she fought against these beliefs: "I had to repeat certain Scriptures a hundred times a day – particularly the ones relating to my identity in Christ, that I was a new creation and that Jesus has qualified me – until they finally started to sink in. It took years before God's promises became the solid foundation of my thought and belief system."

The third time is the charm

Even as Sandra kept herself busy in her job and fought to overcome insecurity, she still involved herself in ministry. And the leaders of her church decided to officially ordain her as a minister to women and young people. That's when God again took action. She describes the experience: "The day I was ordained by my hometown Baptist church, I had the exact same visitation for a *third time*, with the same vision of the church, its components, and the call to start and pastor the church."

Finally, after the third visitation, Sandra was ready and desperate enough to step into it. She blocked out the voices of human beings and listened to God, who told her to "go for it".

After seeing her vision for the third time, Sandra had quite a bit of clarity about her calling, but how would she go about it? Where would she start? And who would come to her church? Nobody was looking for a female preacher to start a new church; in fact, the religious establishment was against her.

Not knowing what else to do, Sandra reached out to the kinds of people Jesus had instructed her to reach: those that most churches didn't want. She went out on the streets and ministered to drug addicts, alcoholics, divorcees, prostitutes, and homosexuals. Many responded to God's love and received healing, which shocked Sandra even as she worked with them. This group of new believers grew rapidly.

Suddenly, she found herself leading a church – and that's how Whole Life Ministries was born.

Death threats and rejection

But growth and progress didn't come without a price. As soon as Whole Life Ministries started to flourish, Sandra began to receive threats of all kinds from people who opposed having women in church leadership positions. Some walked into her services, yelled at her, and tried to physically pull people out of her church.

"Intimidation was a huge issue in the initial stages of pursuing the vision. No one wants people throwing tomatoes at them, and no one wants people to literally rise up against them," Sandra recounts. "I was shocked that the very people I had looked up to came against me. I was very scared and wanted to give up several times." She also received antagonistic letters and even death threats. At one point, it became necessary to investigate the threats by hiring a detective. "I felt alone and was pretty scared," Sandra recalls.

Everybody needs someone to believe in them, and for Sandra it was a man named Dr Kenneth E. Hagin. He reached out and encouraged and mentored her. "If it hadn't been for him, I might have given up," Sandra shares. "Kenneth Hagin had a very different view on the 'woman question', and fully supported me. He became a spiritual father to me and took me under his wing." He kept encouraging her, gave her guidance on dealing with the resistance, and taught her to walk in faith.

Vision has feet

Putting her faith to work was the most important lesson Sandra had to learn in order to walk in her destiny. She explains, "Many people think they have a vision, but they don't understand that vision has hands and feet to it." Having a vision means more than agreeing with it in your mind; you have to cooperate with it. "You can almost compare it with the difference between hope and faith – between just agreeing with something and actually *doing* something. I think that's a missing element for many people," Sandra observes. "The other misunderstanding prevalent among certain church folks is the assumption that God will open doors automatically for the vision to happen and clear any resistance and contradiction out of the way."

The crack in the wall

What helped Sandra deal with the threats, resistance, opposition, and impossible circumstances?

"Through all the difficulties and rejection in the early stages of the ministry, I learned to look for the crack in the wall instead of focusing on the shut door," Sandra explains. "When God speaks, no matter how impossible circumstances seem to be, I know there is always an opening somewhere, and that crack in the wall is going to work for me! I just need to be diligent."

For Sandra, to be diligent means declaring that the opening is there even when everybody says it is not. She says, "I know it's there. It has to be there, or God is not God. You have to realize that God is on your side, that he cares for you, and that he is going to help you follow through with the vision."

Sandra is the first to admit that she has not always seen the crack of possibility. She was stuck in the pit of impossibility. It took several years for her to develop the strength to focus her mind on what is possible and to walk in faith. "Because of all the hardships in the beginning I was forced to decide what I thought about God and his Word. Otherwise I would not have survived. That meant that I kept repeating God's promises to myself over and over again," Sandra explains about her own process. Despite all threats and contradictions, Sandra kept her eyes on the vision.

Today, more than thirty years after launching Whole Life Ministries, the vision is a reality. At 2621 Washington Road in Augusta, Georgia, right across the street from the world-famous Augusta National Golf Course, where the pros play every year in the Masters Tournament, you'll find The Master's Plaza in front of the large campus of Whole Life Ministries. In its healing centre people are taught the Word of God and receive ministry for healing. It has a large sanctuary, offices, a TV studio with an international broadcasting ministry, a bookshop, an elementary school, and a café – all in the exact layout and design that Sandra saw in her three identical visions decades before.

Contradiction of reality

Sandra is thankful that her vision is now a reality, but she admits that there were many times while establishing the ministry when she felt incredibly discouraged. At the same time, she has also had amazing supernatural breakthroughs, and her secret for walking in victory and overcoming feelings of discouragement has been to stay focused on those breakthroughs.

She explains that she knows she needs to keep talking about God's miracles. "I know my secret for walking in victory is to stay in awe of God. To remember what he did there – and then expect him to do it again in any new situation that also looks impossible. I know my key is to stay fascinated by him and I focus on that." Sandra sees a miracle every day, because she has trained her mind that way. Even as most people don't recognize what God is doing, Sandra does. She reminds herself of what God is doing and talks about it continually. That helps her deal with the contradictions.

"Take the example of Abraham and all the contradictions he was facing," Sandra elaborates. "He had a promise, but there was nothing in his circumstances that agreed with it. I've been in that situation so many times, and I believe that's where a lot of people are. You have a certain dream and vision in your heart, and then everything looks full of contradictions."

She continues, *"But you cannot keep looking at the promise and the contradiction at the same time.* It's impossible. The contradictions seem so huge and the promise so small. But in the end, it all boils down to this one issue: you have to determine the integrity of God's Word. You have to decide what you believe about God, because this is what you end up with.

This is what God said on the one hand – and this is what it looks like on the other. So you have to decide: is this the truth?"

Sandra describes her breakthrough: "Once I finally got to the point where I believed that what God said was the truth, I could process the contradictions. If what God said was the truth it could not end up the way it all looked. I know God is there; I know he won't leave me." However, Sandra is honest enough to admit that this doesn't mean she never wonders whether God is on a sabbatical. "I do ask him, 'Where are you? I can't find you! I know you are here, because you said you are here, but I wish you would somehow make it known to me.' I do say, 'Don't you realize I'm sinking? So you'd better come through real fast. I'm counting on you, because you are unchangeable, and you cannot lie.' And he always does, because God is faithful."

The truth question

When faced with heavy contradictions and disappointments, many people abandon their dreams, visions, and callings. Sandra says, "I think people get caught up in their own things, and I understand that. I get caught up in a lot of things. I have difficulties, I have trials, and I have to conquer all kinds of thoughts and emotions."

Sometimes Sandra ends up burying a person she has prayed for and believed would be healed. At other times she experiences feelings of discouragement, fear, or frustration. And she goes through times where she does not hear God's voice or feel his presence. But again, for her it all comes back to this question: *is this truth*? She explains, "The contradictions look very real to me, and they contradict what God said. The circumstances contradict the promise, and the promise contradicts the circumstances. There is no middle ground."

How does she handle it?

"I come back to what God said and go over it again and again. I say to him, 'If you said this, you have to do it.' And I receive peace. I might be troubled again the next day, and then I have to go over it again. But it's ultimately the Word and who God is. You have to determine whether you believe that what God said is the truth."

Not fitting the pattern

In order to follow her vision, Sandra has had to conquer the fear of man, the urge to try to win everyone's approval, and her own insecurity and timidity. She has had to face resistance, ridicule, threats, and rejection while walking out the vision.

But the greatest challenge through all the years in walking in the vision has been doing it as an unmarried woman. Sandra describes the feeling: "I've taken bold steps against all kinds of things, taken a stand and also said a lot of controversial things – but the hardest for me when all's said and done is that I walk into my house alone. This was a real issue I had with God.

Sandra never intended to stay single, but in not compromising on the vision, she paid a price and lost the prospect of marriage. She was engaged to be married more than once, but disagreements always came up around the issue of her being the lead pastor. Faced with the choice between remaining lead pastor – as her vision had clearly compelled her to do – and marrying the man, she chose to follow the vision.

Sandra admits that she still struggles with this contradiction, and the loneliness that it brings. "The loneliness is incomprehensible. What most people don't understand is that it's tough as a single person to deal with the fact that everybody is going to their houses and doing things with their families and you're not included. The feeling of being left out can be very painful. You come home and you are alone. There's nobody there with you to share the troubles or to celebrate the victories. There's nobody there to tell you that everything is going to be all right when you are in the thick of it."

Finding people who understand and identify with her is a struggle for Sandra. She laments, "Many married people say they understand, but they have no earthly idea. For one thing, most married people don't know how to identify with a single person – and then with me in particular, because I don't fit the pattern. I don't fit the pattern of what a preacher should be, because I'm a woman – and then I don't fit the pattern of what a woman should be, because I am very politically minded and involved in what's going on in the world. I would rather sit with the men and discuss current issues."

How does she cope with this isolation? Sandra continues to focus on her experiences where she has felt God's nearness. "What has helped me overcome the feelings of loneliness was and still is to focus on the amazing miracles that have happened: we have seen eight brain-dead people get healed; we've had countless miraculous interventions in people's lives," she shares.

They have seen every kind of miracle, from the healing of terminal diseases such as cancer to freedom from addictions. They've seen restored marriages, financial provision, and sudden job openings.

Sandra continues, "We've had supernatural signs in our services, such as the drums playing while nobody was sitting at the drum set, and winds blowing through the sanctuary while the air conditioning was turned off. I keep talking about these things, because that's my secret to victory: getting excited about who God is, staying in tune with what God is doing, staying awestruck about it. Talking about it is what enables me to face all the resistance and still pursue the vision. It makes me deal with the singleness; it makes me deal with discouragement and hard things. I just keep talking like a child about it."

The secret to victorious living

It is important that each person finds the secret that keeps them in victory, and talking about God's miracles is one of Sandra's keys to victory. "I remember one time I complained to God that I was not in victory, and he replied, 'Then do what you were doing when you were in victory.' That is what I try to do."

This is her advice for gaining the upper hand in the face of any struggle or contradiction: "Whatever your secret to your victory is, find out what it is and go back to it. I can guarantee that something is going to change. But you have to know your secret to victory, and that entails constantly having to think about it and focus your mind on it."

When studying the lives of many victorious individuals throughout history, this pattern can always be observed: they knew their secret, and that was the key to their victory. How else could they have dealt with unspeakable pain, loss, humiliation, and unimaginable atrocities? It was all because they knew their secret.

The secret, however, varies between individuals. For instance, for Corrie Ten Boom, the secret to victory was forgiveness. For Victor Frankl, it was a practice of visualization and holding the future in front of him. For Mother Teresa, the key that strengthened her was meditation. Dietrich Bonhoeffer found singing old hymns was a source of comfort that sustained him in his time of imprisonment.

This is to name just a few. Do you know what your secret is? Do you know your key to victory? Knowing your secret makes you more resilient in the battle. It doesn't mean you won't get hurt, weary, or discouraged, but when you do, you will not give up – you will get up again. You will continue to pursue your destiny and focus your vision on the promise instead of the contradiction.

Chapter Seven
Faith Under Fire

Torn between agony and ecstasy

Canon Andrew White

People often say to me, "Take care."
But I say to them, "Take risks!"
Canon Andrew White, Vicar Emeritus of Baghdad

A vital article of clothing in Andrew White's wardrobe in Baghdad was a heavy bulletproof vest. On a particular summer day in 2008, he wore the vest as he left the secure Green Zone. Like many other days, he was on his way to meet a middleman for hostage negotiation. When he met with terrorists, he usually wore his Anglican collar shirt underneath the body armour. When he met high officials, ayatollahs, ministers, and presidents, or when visiting members of his congregation in one of the bombed and forlorn districts of Baghdad, he usually wore a suit with one of his extravagant, colourful bow ties. These items – minus the body armour – are his trademark even today.

It was an excruciatingly hot July day in Baghdad. Wearing the heavy vest was insufferable in the heat, but it was necessary. Andrew's security guards insisted on it. "Negotiating with kidnappers is a dangerous business!" they reminded him, but none of them expected that later that day they would experience this first-hand. As they set out to negotiate the release of a kidnapped victim, they had no idea they would be kidnapped themselves.

"It all happened so quickly," Andrew related to me in our interview in a surprisingly calm, everyday tone. "I was dozing as we were driving in the convoy across the desert, when all of a sudden our car was halted. Suddenly I woke up with an AK47 pointing at my face and a guy with a scarf wrapped around his head demanding all our money. Our driver wanted to escape, but I told him they would kill us if we tried to run."

Andrew can assess a situation pretty quickly and accurately, and his instinct was that these people were not to be trifled with. "Once, an Israeli soldier pointed a gun at my face, and I told him to stop that nonsense and grow up," he says about a less-dangerous encounter. "He was just an inexperienced young chap." This time Andrew sensed a threat of a totally different dimension.

The terrorist took their money, but he didn't let them go. Instead, Andrew was taken hostage and thrown onto the floor of a bare cell, where he quickly realized he was surrounded by severed fingers and toes.

At that point, he told me in a dry, matter-of-fact voice, he got "a bit worried" about his fingers, so he started to pray. "Lord, what am I going to do? I need my fingers to write!" Reflexively, he put his hands in his pockets. To his surprise, he found in one a handful of money – a donation he had received earlier for his work and promptly forgot. He was delighted to find nearly $2,000 in his pocket now. He chuckles at the memory, in spite of the danger he was in.

"I gave the money to the kidnapper, and he let me go."

Armed and dangerous

Andrew affirms that he was only worried in this hostage situation about his fingers, which reveals one of the unique features of his personality. "I've always been fearless and calm-headed; it's not something I've developed or grown into."

He is armed with fearlessness, and this trait enables him to enter enemy territory and do his work of peace negotiation, but his security guards also remind him that it is his greatest pitfall. He simply has no concept of fear or danger, so his security guards in Baghdad have a busy job keeping him safe.

Andrew White is a sagacious character, and his unique, amiable, and cheerful personality has won him friends even among the most unfriendly and hostile participants in the religious and political conflict currently occurring in the Middle East. As Director of the International Centre of Reconciliation of the Anglican Church in England, Andrew has become an anchor in the storm for leaders and foreign ministers in the Middle East, and an indispensable source of information for Washington and Downing Street on the political and religious conflicts there.

Andrew has often been called in for highly sensitive hostage negotiations in the war zones of the Middle East. For example, he was the key negotiator during the siege of the Church of the Nativity in Bethlehem in 2002. His incredible insight and understanding of the nature of the conflict, and his relentless efforts to bring enemies around one table and listen to each other's pain and suffering, has won him the trust of opposing parties in the Middle East.

Andrew has been a confidant to former Israeli Deputy Foreign Minister Michael Melchior for many years. And in the 1980s, he also became a close friend to Yasser Arafat, even though he did not agree with his political views. He explains why – and how – he does it: "In peace negotiations, you have to listen to both sides and understand where they are coming from. If everyone you were dealing with was nice there wouldn't be any wars. Nice people usually don't start wars. Being friends with not-so-nice people is essential in peace negotiations. Loving your enemies then becomes very real!"

In loving his enemies, Andrew went as far as to extend a dinner invitation to some of the top Islamic State leaders in Iraq, to see if there might be a way to work toward reconciliation. But they let Andrew know that if they were to come for dinner, they would chop off his head. Andrew describes his response with his customary dry British humour: "Then I decided to withdraw my dinner invitation and not have them over." He then turns very serious. "Unfortunately, there are people you cannot work with, and ISIS belongs to that category."

Becoming a history maker

Andrew's intelligence and understanding brought him into a significant position at a remarkably young age. He took the position as Canon at the International Ministry of Coventry Cathedral at the age of thirty-three. It is very unusual to be appointed as Canon in the Anglican Church under the age of thirty-five, but Andrew's insight and experience in peace negotiations convinced the board he was the best candidate for the intricate task ahead.

"I'm not a clever guy; I really am not that bright!" Andrew insists. "My parents always said, 'Andrew has a really nice personality, but he's not very bright.'" Nevertheless, he has seventeen doctorates. "But I only have three real doctorates," he smiles. "The rest are pretend ones – but they are actually the nice ones, because you don't have to work for them." Nowadays, he turns down most of the honorary doctorates offered to him, unless they are from really strategic places. Andrew's first earned doctorate is in medicine, his second is in theology, and the third is in Judaism.

"You can only do one thing"

When Andrew was ten years old, his schoolteacher asked him what he wanted to be when he was older.

"I want to be an anaesthesiologist and a priest!" he said.

His teacher replied, "You can't do both, Andrew. You can only do one thing."

But if you tell Andrew White that something cannot be done, he will prove you wrong.

"My teacher said that I couldn't be a priest because my father was a Calvinist and my mother was a Pentecostal, and there they don't have priests. So I became an Anglican!" he jokes.

Even though Andrew's personality has always been bright, cheerful, and easy-going, his journey has not always been as easy as he often makes it seem. "I didn't really turn out to be bright until I was in my final year of school," Andrew explains. "That year I was in hospital for nine months, because I had lymphosarcoma. I was undergoing cancer treatment, and I had to do all my advanced level exams on my own."

During his treatment, he fell in love with St Thomas' Hospital and soon decided that all he wanted to do in life was work at that very same hospital. Considering his circumstances, this didn't seem very likely, but his passion for medicine drove him to high performance. He passed his A levels with flying colours.

Passion fuels excellence

"Here is the key," Andrew points out emphatically. "I'm bright when I'm *passionate* about something. Things I'm not passionate about, even if I really should be, I'm no good at. Passion drives me to excellence. And all I could think about when I was undergoing cancer treatment was that I wanted to do my medical training as an anaesthetist at St Thomas' Hospital."

The reality is that cancer was one of the lesser illnesses in Andrew's personal medical history. As a child, he developed serious ear problems as a result of infections and other complications. During his teenage years, he underwent dozens of operations in an attempt to alleviate the pain. That's when he developed a fascination with anaesthesiology. As a twelve-year-old, he devoured medical textbooks. Then, the next time he needed to be on the operating table, he gave instructions to the doctors and nurses. The medical staff thought they were dealing with a teenage smart alec, but soon they were dumbfounded by his extensive and detailed medical knowledge.

A storybook career

Andrew's childhood and teenage medical issues were minor compared to the disappointment he experienced when his dream of becoming an anaesthesiologist at St Thomas' Hospital seemed to be shattered. "One day the letter arrived – and it said I had *not* been accepted. I was devastated!" Andrew remembers. "I had lived and studied and prepared for this one option. That was probably the day of the biggest discouragement in my life." The fact that he had been accepted for medical training at another hospital was of no consolation to him at that point. His greatest dream had been destroyed. Or at least it appeared to have been.

While Andrew was still trying to come to terms with his disappointment, something very unusual happened. He describes it: "A week later I received another letter from St Thomas' Hospital, stating that they had made a mistake and that I was accepted for medical training after all. And they asked if I would please forgive them for the mix-up. But I didn't need to forgive them – I loved them! God had rescued my dream."

Andrew started his medical training at the age of seventeen, and his passion for medicine drove him to a high level of performance. His one ambition in life was to run the cardiac arrest team at St Thomas', and he hoped to achieve this goal by the age of thirty. However, owing to some issues within the cardiac arrest team, Andrew was actually put in charge of it at the age of twenty-four. It was a storybook career and more than he had ever dared to dream of.

But then something happened which would totally disrupt his plans and change the course of his life forever.

"I still remember that day as clear as yesterday," Andrew recounts. "I was in my private room at St Thomas' and expressing my gratefulness to God for having given me everything I had ever dreamed of. I was working at the place I had always wanted to and was doing what I had always wanted to do, so I was thanking God for all of it. And then I remembered the words of a preacher, that when you have achieved all you have wanted to achieve, you should ask God what's next. So I did. I asked, 'What's next, Lord?' and he answered promptly, 'I want you to become a priest in the Anglican church.'"

Andrew goes on, "I was shocked. I argued with God and said, 'The Anglican Church? Do you know they are not even all *saved*?'

"And he said, 'Of course I do.'

"I continued to reason with God and said I would not be really good at being a priest. And why should I leave a career that I was really good at? It didn't make sense at all, and I didn't want to give up my dream, so I fought him. It lasted for exactly half an hour, and then I realized you cannot win an argument with God. So I said, 'Okay.'"

Laying down his dream

Saying something and then actually following it through are two different things. But Andrew did go all the way through with it. Against the advice of his parents, friends, and superiors, he resigned from the job he so loved, packed up his belongings, and left the safe haven of his splendid career. He then applied to the "vicar factory" – as he calls the school of theology – at

Cambridge. He followed the call to travel in a new direction, but it would not be a smooth ride.

"Studying theology was hard," Andrew says. "My medical training was nothing compared to the disciplines in theology I had to master. I found it extremely challenging and very difficult. And on top of it, I found the Christian theology extremely boring. The only subject I was interested in was Judaism – and eventually I went to Israel to study Judaism."

Andrew was the first non-Jew – or *goy*, as they would call him – to study at a Jewish Yeshiva (a traditional Jewish seminary). "I totally loved it," Andrew shares. "You can only understand Judaism when you actually live it, and that's what I did. I loved the Hasidic tradition – a very conservative orthodox stream in Judaism – and I became even more Hasidic than the Orthodox Jews themselves."

It was then and there that Andrew learned first-hand about the problems and conflicts in the Middle East. In fact, the insights he gained while living there would be of incredible value to his future work. He completed his third doctorate, in Judaism, and then returned to England to serve his curacy in Clapham, London.

Andrew was no regular curate. During his first years of theological studies at Cambridge, he had become involved in the work of the International Council of Christians and Jews (ICCJ). So when he returned from Israel, he was asked to take on a senior role and continue with the work of Jewish–Christian relations. In addition to serving his parish, he would be travelling all over the world and addressing international concerns. He would pop over to the Vatican to visit Pope John Paul II, with whom he would develop a close friendship, fly to the Middle East, travel throughout England and Europe, and on Sundays deliver his sermon to his country parish. It was by no means an average curacy.

Diagnosed with MS

From his local parish, Andrew was called to apply for a highly
significant senior position within the Church of England, as
Director of International Ministry at the International Centre
for Reconciliation. But as soon as he started this intense work,
he developed serious problems with his balance and his vision.
He had not yet made even one overseas trip in his new position
within the Church of England when he was admitted to hospital
and had to undergo a number of complicated neurological tests,
including a lumbar puncture to test his cerebral spinal fluid.
These tests would confirm the preliminary diagnosis: multiple
sclerosis (MS). When the doctor came with the test results,
Andrew was shattered.

It was very depressing, but he did not have time to shed
many tears. Within two hours of hearing the news, Andrew had
to change his mindset from that of being a patient to being a
husband, for his wife was on the way to hospital, about to give
birth to their second son.

Andrew describes how he processed the medical news: "It's
always been like that in my life: agony and ecstasy go hand in
hand. I actually couldn't dwell long on the diagnosis and the
fact that I had MS, because I was thrown right away into the
excitement of the birth of our second son!"

Andrew's medical problems have been significant challenges
in his life. And yet these issues haven't stopped him. "I can only
say for myself that my faith and trust in God have always been
very simple. I have always loved him in a very simple way, and
it has never changed. I have never doubted. That has carried me
through my challenges."

Andrew has faced his challenges by focusing on holding the
course and doing what needs to be done. "When I was dealing
with cancer in my youth, and the terrible pain in my ears,
I just had to keep putting one foot in front of the other and

simply live each day at a time. Since MS was added to the list of medical challenges, I've just had to keep taking all of these tablets," Andrew says, speaking of the large arsenal of pills that he has to take several times a day.

Andrew's lighthearted and cheerful personality has helped him deal with the extreme challenges of his health issues. However, he says that if he had focused on the problems, he would have become depressed, just as many other people do who are dealing with similar problems. But there is one key that helps him deal with the challenges: "Despite all these health issues, I have actually never thought of myself as being ill."

From hospital bed to hostage negotiation

Andrew knows that his positive personality and optimistic outlook on life are a blessing. He celebrates life and gets on with the tasks ahead, but at the same time he makes an effort to focus on the positive. Andrew demonstrates this focus, saying, "The positive thing is that I have only had two times when I was taken into hospital with my MS." He chooses not to think about all the times he has not felt well.

On one of his bad days, Andrew was lying in a hospital bed when he received a phone call from Yasser Arafat. "*Abuna* [Father], they have taken my church! I need you to come quickly!"

Andrew replied, "Look, I'm a bit tied up at the moment. I'm in hospital – I can't come."

But Arafat insisted. "No, I need you; they've got my church!"

This was in 2002, when the Israel Defense Forces (IDF) occupied Bethlehem to capture Palestinian militants. When the terrorists realized they were surrounded, they fled into the Church of the Nativity, which was then surrounded by the Israeli military. A standoff ensued.

Because of the severity of his illness, again Andrew declined to go. But that call was followed immediately by two more: one from the Israeli Deputy Minister of Foreign Affairs and the next from the Archbishop of Canterbury.

"It became clear that I was the only person trusted by both sides involved in this conflict," Andrew recounts. "So I saw no other option but to discharge myself from hospital and fly over there."

The negotiations presented an extremely complex and delicate challenge because, along with the terrorists, a large number of Palestinian civilians had fled into the church. Now they and the monks in charge of the property were being held captive too. Around 200 lives were in danger, and Andrew felt the weight of responsibility for their lives on his shoulders.

"For thirty-nine days we were in negotiations, and for the first fifteen we were negotiating how to negotiate," Andrew remembers.

After many endless negotiations and sleepless nights, a resolution was achieved. Sadly, the entire affair was not without casualties: eight Palestinians were killed during the siege, and an Armenian monk and several Israeli soldiers were severely wounded.

It was not until Andrew returned to England that he discovered the magnitude of what had been achieved. Suddenly, he was a celebrated hero in the British newspapers as the successful hostage negotiator. It was at that point that his suppressed emotions surfaced. "I realized that from now on my life would be a bittersweet mixture of agony and ecstasy, of terrible lows as well as joyous highs – and I wondered if I could really live with such trauma," Andrew writes in his book, *My Journey So Far*.[1] It took some time and professional counselling to process the traumatic event, but Andrew concludes that the whole experience helped him to see his own vulnerability and how much he must rely on God for his grace and power in his life. "I realized that in my own strength, I can't do it. I need God every day," he writes.[2]

Treating MS in the war zone

Despite all his health challenges, Andrew continues to operate at a high level of international leadership. Has he ever wondered why God has not healed him, considering that he has such a difficult task and calling?

"No, I've never thought that way," Andrew explains. "Some people told me that if I had enough faith God would do a miracle and heal me. *But the real miracle is actually that I've been able to do everything I need to do!* And I get on with it. That's the amazing thing to me."

Not that it has always been easy or painless. Early in his ministry in Iraq, he experienced a severe flare-up in his multiple sclerosis. He recounts, "My MS symptoms kept getting worse every day, until I could not move at all any more and just lay on my bed. I would lose my balance and fall over as soon as I got up, and my vision was blurred. It was pretty depressing."

Cure from a Google search

"One day, one of my Iraqi doctors came to me and told me that he had found a method which would help me get better," says Andrew.

The doctor went on to describe the treatment he was recommending. "You need a stem cell treatment," he explained.

Andrew immediately interrupted him. "I know about stem cell treatment, but you know that I can't do that. I won't take embryo stem cells – it violates my ethics."

"No, I'm talking about your own stem cells," the doctor said. He went on to explain that there was a new machine that would be able to extract the stem cells from a person's own blood.

"Really? Does it work?"

"Yeah, I've googled it!"

"That's how things work in Baghdad!" Andrew recounts. Because he was always up for pioneering and doing experiments, he agreed to the unusual treatment. With the help of the US Embassy, the hospital was able to obtain the machine. And Andrew, with his own medical experience, assisted in the procedure. "I placed the peripheral venous catheter myself and administered my own therapy, so I could play doctor again," he describes.

Even today, this type of stem cell treatment is only performed in a few countries. In Iraq, a treatment programme that was launched to help Andrew has now turned the hospital in Baghdad into an important centre for treating MS. More than 2,000 people have travelled to Baghdad from various parts of the world to receive this successful treatment. And, as with Andrew, the stem cell treatment has greatly improved their quality of life. "Since the treatment, I've become much better," says Andrew. "Apart from some balance problems, I am doing fine."

Making things happen

When it comes to being a pioneer, Andrew White is always up for it. He is known as a mover and shaker. "I assess the situation, and then I go and make it happen," he says. "For instance, one of my people needs radical surgery. I know the doctor who can do it, and I can organize it. What I need is the money. So I'll find the money and I'll make it happen! That's the reality."

It's in the practical steps and taking action where many people fail. In addition, many Christians operate out of a false spirituality, believing that taking action is somehow unspiritual, and that waiting on God means that he will make it happen. But as Andrew explains, "We have to work with God in making things happen – otherwise we are just wasting our time. It's not that opportunities are not there. *You have to see everything as a God-given opportunity. But in those opportunities, you always have to make things happen!*"

Andrew lives out what he advises. His access to world leaders and the influence they allow him to have has not always been presented to him on a silver platter. Sometimes, opportunities have simply presented themselves. But more often than not, Andrew has gone out of his way to get to know key players.

Andrew also went out of his way to gain access into Iraq while Saddam Hussein's regime was still in power. At the time, Britain had no diplomatic relations with the closed country. Andrew tried everything to obtain permission to visit Iraq, with no success. He could have given up when faced with all the apparent "closed doors". Instead, he gathered his team to pray that God would make a way.

The very next day, Andrew received a formal invitation to visit the country from Saddam Hussein's former deputy, Tariq Aziz. He eagerly went, and over his following visits he gained favour and trust among the leaders and the people. Eventually, he was able to move to Baghdad, where he revived the ministry of St George's – the only Anglican church in the city, which had been closed down after the 1991 war in Iraq.

Joy in the midst of persecution

Andrew describes the situation in Iraq. "Saddam Hussein's regime was evil. The country was shattered into pieces and the population was suffering terribly." But he goes on to explain that what has happened since the US military left Iraq and ISIS took over is 100 times worse than Saddam's regime ever was. "People get massacred every day, Muslims as well as Christians," he says. Years ago, the whole Christian community fled the city of Mosul (Nineveh of ancient times) and went to Baghdad to escape the impending approach of ISIS. Unfortunately, now ISIS has infiltrated Baghdad as well. There's not a single member in his congregation who has not experienced the loss of a family member or friend to the onslaught of ISIS. Their lives are in continual danger.

What the people in Baghdad – and Christians in particular – are going through is totally foreign to the Western experience. Andrew describes one such situation: "One day Yusef, one of the members of our congregation, called me and he was very upset."

Crying, the man asked, "*Abuna*, will Jesus still love me?"

Andrew asked him what had happened.

"Today the ISIS came to my house, and they said if I did not say the words of Mohammed the prophet, they would kill my children!" he cried. "I could not bear to see my children killed, so I said the words. Will Jesus forgive me?"

"I assured him that Jesus would never stop loving him," Andrew says. But, he concludes, "That is what our people are facing every day."

Tragically, only a week later, the members of ISIS returned to Yusef's house when he was not there and the children were alone with their mother. They demanded that the children say the prayer to convert to Islam, but the children refused. They said, "We will never leave *Yeshua* [Jesus]! He is everything to us. How could we leave him?" And ISIS killed all four children before their mother's eyes.

We Westerners can hardly conceive of such a horrible situation, but it is these people's reality. Yet in the midst of the horrors, Andrew testifies that the Christian community in Baghdad is one of the *happiest* places he has ever known. "There is great joy among our people because we have each other. We stick together, we laugh together, and we cry together. We really love each other and are very close. We are like one family." It is the suffering that brings them together, and in that unity they find their comfort and strength. Andrew concludes, "The reality is that when everybody is being crushed, you have to stick together. You've got no choice."

Andrew also explains that in the face of such extreme hardship and persecution, Jesus becomes very real. "You realize that Jesus is the only hope. When you have lost everything, Jesus is all you've got, and that's why they are happy, because they have nothing left but Jesus. It's amazing, but our people are extremely grateful. When you've lost everything, you're grateful even for nothing."

Suffering and glory

One might wonder how this is possible. How can you live and even be joyful in the midst of such suffering?

"Suffering and glory are linked together," Andrew explains. "I don't think you can ever see real glory unless you have suffered. Romans 8:17 says that unless you have experienced the suffering of the cross, you cannot know the glory of the cross. So we have known the suffering, but we also know the glory of the cross."

When I asked him to give an example of the glory they see, Andrew states in a dry, matter-of-fact voice, "Well, there is the resurrection of the dead."

And that's the only thing he gives away. It takes some probing to get more details on that – but that is Andrew White. No hype, no puffing up; simple and down to earth. But here is one such story:

"I still remember the day when Ahmed came to our medical clinic. He wanted his daughter to be treated by our doctors, because she wasn't getting any better in the state hospital. We had to tell him that we could not treat a patient who was already in another hospital. I prayed for Ahmed and his daughter, and I felt the Lord say he would heal her. So I instructed Ahmed to go back to the hospital and pray for his daughter," Andrew recalls.

But when Ahmed returned to the state hospital, the doctors there told him that his daughter had died. Desperately, Ahmed ran to her hospital room, put his arms around her, and said, "Yeshua!" over and over again.

Suddenly, his daughter breathed out, sat up, and said, "*Baba* [Daddy], I'm hungry. Can I have some food?"

Andrew continues, "Later, when Ahmed came to see me and told me what had happened I simply said, 'Don't worry, it has happened before.'"

Love casts out all fear

After these glorious experiences, is Andrew's faith invincible, or has it ever been under fire? "It's under fire all the time," Andrew says. "But I've never been drawn to the point of doubting. Yes, we do see incredible miracles, but they don't happen all the time."

Andrew describes what sustains him: "It's the love of my children in Baghdad. There is so much strength in the unity of our people, and the children in particular – the ones we have taken in and adopted. Love casts out all fear, and when you truly love each other, you find comfort and strength."

This comfort was in evidence when Yusef's four children were killed. "I was shattered and sobbing in my study," says Andrew. "But then our children who live with us at the centre came to me and said, 'Daddy, don't cry, because we saw them. They are in heaven, dancing with Jesus.' And that really gave me strength and helped me to take comfort. That is where we find strength, because love casts out all fear."

After experiencing so many shattered hopes, do the people in the war zone still have hopes and dreams for the future? Yes, they do. "The hopes and dreams of the children are very simple: to be able to study and achieve at school, to be able to go to university, and eventually to marry the right person," Andrew shares. As for the adults, their hopes are that one day they will be able to live in peace. But at this point, all they can do is wait. Andrew explains, "Sometimes the children ask me, 'When will there be peace?' And I have to say that God's timing is not like our timing. The problem is that Jesus said he would come back soon – and that is now 2,000 years ago."

A new chapter

Tragically, the violence and terror of ISIS in and around Baghdad has increased exponentially. Most Christians have fled the country and now reside in refugee camps in Lebanon and Jordan. As for Andrew, his work eventually attracted the attention of ISIS and made him one of their most-wanted targets. In 2014, Archbishop of Canterbury Justin Welby ordered him to leave Baghdad. Welby the view expressed that Andrew would be of more value alive than dead.

For Andrew, who had declared that he would never leave his people, this was a very difficult decision. He had lived and ministered in Baghdad for more than ten years. But in the end, he abided by the Archbishop's decision and returned to England. He still visits Baghdad frequently, but underground and unannounced. His main work is still among Iraqi Christians, but it has relocated to Jordan, where most of them fled. There he has established another centre, much like the one in Baghdad, which provides housing, education, and health care for the refugees.

Andrew's unique life story might give the impression that he is a spiritual superhero, but he would say that nothing is further from the truth. He is constantly confronted with his own weaknesses and limitations, and his physical difficulties have been a thorn in his flesh that God has not removed. Since our interview,

Andrew's physical problems have increased. His intense MS symptoms have inhibited him severely since he has not been able to obtain entry clearance to travel to Baghdad to receive the stem cell treatment that the hospital still offers. Often dependent on a wheelchair now, he finds himself even more totally dependent on God and others. But in the midst of his dependency, he continues to move forward and make things happen.

Andrew's personality, passion, and professional skill flow together and find perfect expression in the position God has called him to. He does what he does from a place of authenticity, and not out of performance-oriented striving or selfish pursuit of fame. His character and gifting continue to make him the right person for this job.

The most important key to dealing with suffering and obstacles, however, is found in the persecuted church. Their love, their unity, and their fellowship hold them together and invite the presence of God in such a way that they not only share in the suffering of Christ, but also experience his glory. Once again, it's in the midst of contradictions and losses that Jesus is revealed and his presence becomes tangible. And yes, in Baghdad, sometimes the people are so afraid that they don't dare leave their houses for days. "But when we encourage one another and love one another, fear loses its grip," Andrew says.

Sometimes dreams don't work out the way we hoped or imagined. But Andrew's life is a demonstration of turning every situation into an opportunity to follow the path of the dream, even if obstacles on the way demand a detour. He always looks at the positive and focuses on the opportunities. "I always say I learned as much about life in the operating theatre as I did in the theatre of war. And I have loved both. I love the adrenaline and excitement – that's part of my personality," Andrew continues. "But no matter where you are, if you want to fulfil your destiny, you have to step out. People often say to me, 'Take care,' but I say to them, 'Take risks!'"

This is one of the greatest life lessons Andrew has learned, and it is one of the greatest lessons we can gather from his story to overcome the obstacles we are facing and succeed in life. If we want to walk out more of our destiny, we would do well to heed Andrew White's main advice: "Don't take care; take risks!"

Chapter Eight
Inside *The Shack*

Dealing with the wounds of the soul

William Paul Young

> Success is becoming a truly authentic person. True
> success is the overflow of authenticity, or else it's not
> success. Else it's just another façade.
>
> *William Paul Young*

It was a dreary, rainy afternoon in Portland, Oregon. Paul travelled along the highway in dense traffic on the way to his office. Dark clouds released a torrent of thick, heavy raindrops that deluged his windshield. The wipers, working at top speed, could not keep up with the relentless downpour. The onslaught of water blurred the glass and his vision. The road became slippery, and he had to slow down.

He reflected that this was a perfect illustration of his life. No matter how hard he worked, no matter how much he tried to wipe away the residue of his past and get a grip on his life, a dark cloud of shame and sadness followed him, dousing him in a downpour that overwhelmed him and blurred his vision. He felt weary, disillusioned, exhausted, and completely lost.

A few minutes earlier, while sitting with a friend at lunch, his phone had rung. It was Kim, his wife. When her name appeared on his mobile phone and the familiar ring sounded, he did what he usually did: he pulled himself together and played the game he calls "Let's pretend everything is fine and under control".

"What's up?" he asked, clueless about the storm that was about to hit him.

"I am waiting for you in your office, And I KNOW!" An explosion of fury blasted through the phone. It made his head spin and his ears tingle. Click. She was gone.

Paul froze. He knew exactly what she *knew*. A rush of thoughts swirled through his mind: "How could she have found out? How am I going to explain?" But there was no way to explain this, no excuse that could save him. He had already told too many lies, and this time he had been caught. This was it – he was finished.

"I have to leave," he told his friend, and he hurried to his car and took off. He didn't even know where he was going – he just needed to get away.

Now, as the rain doused his windshield and made it impossible to see, he decided to pull off the road. He turned off the wipers and sat, frozen, in his car, staring into the forlorn nothingness of a deluge of rain. "The best thing is just to kill myself. There is no way out of *this*," he reasoned.

He picked up his phone and called *her*.

"Let's run!" she suggested.

The thought had already crossed his mind, but he knew that it was what he'd always done: run. And he was tired of it.

"No. I can't do this any more," Paul said in a numb voice. "I've been running all my life. I'm done running. I have to face this."

He hung up. Then he realized that with the last five words he had just ruled out another of his options: to kill himself. That, after all, would be the ultimate way to run – and never to return.

Robotically, Paul started his car and pulled back onto the highway. Everything was still a blur.

He didn't know how he made it there, but finally he found himself in front of his office. His heart was racing, his chest tight, and he felt the blood pulsing through his veins as he walked up to the door. Grabbing the knob, he hesitated. "Am I really going to do this? Killing myself would be the easier way out." Once more he weighed his options. But he opened the door and walked into his office.

Kim had torn it apart. Papers and books were on the floor; drawers had been emptied and the contents spread across the room. As she came toward him, he prepared for the fury that would assail him without mercy.

"You hypocrite! You liar! How could you do this to me?" she ranted, pounding his chest with her fists. "How could you betray me with my best friend?" she shouted. "I trusted you! What other secrets are you hiding from me?"

She had no idea... But somehow, this time Paul knew that he would have to tell her EVERYTHING.

The jungle kid

It had all started in the jungle of Irian Jaya – or even before that – with his parents. The young married couple, still in their early twenties, were sent out as missionaries by a conservative evangelical denomination. They travelled to their mission field: an unreached, stone-age cannibalistic tribe in the highlands of West Papua, once Netherlands, New Guinea. With little training or preparation for the assignment ahead, the Youngs ventured out with their ten-month-old son Paul and began their work in the middle of a hostile jungle environment.

From the beginning, the ministry was overwhelming, and Paul's parents were immediately consumed by work. Left to play outside, Paul grew up among the tribe, and it became his family, practically raising him. Because the tribe was more friendly to the child than to the parents, Paul also grew up as a kind of go-between for them and the *white men*. In addition, his father was a very angry and harsh man, so Paul understood from an early age that "home" and "father" were not safe to be around.

Paul's parents belonged to a generation that didn't know they were carrying any emotional baggage, and if they had known, they wouldn't have known what to do with it. The teachings of their fundamental evangelical denomination, which encouraged a detachment from emotions along with the sacrificing of everything on God's altar, reinforced a stoic and emotionless approach to life. In addition, Paul's father had come from a broken background and carried a lot of unresolved anger. Paul learned from his example to run and hide from his own fear and pain.

By the age of four, Paul was fluent in both the *Dani* dialect and English. With those skills, he was a valuable source for a Wycliffe Bible translator who was studying the language in order to translate the New Testament. As such, he was a valuable "instrument" for the "work of God" – but he paid a high price for that.

Dark rituals

For young Paul, becoming a part of the tribe was a way to belong, and also to be away from his father. The tribe taught him how to hunt, how to survive in the jungle, and how to carve and shoot arrows. In his mind, he was a *Dani* and a member of the family tribe. Present when tribal members discussed whether to kill his parents, the *ghost people*, Paul felt no fear. He wasn't even conscious that he himself was white. His identity and sense of belonging were rooted in the tribal culture of the *Dani* people.

But from his *Dani* family, it wasn't only useful skills like surviving in the jungle and speaking the tribal dialect that Paul learned. This tribal culture was highly sexualized, and he was introduced to the darkness of childhood sexual abuse at the age of four. He would hide this secret for years to come.

The abuse happened frequently, sometimes only ten or fifteen feet away from his parents, who were busy and preoccupied with the mission work. Paul himself hid the abuse from them because he knew that something was wrong, and he believed it was his fault. He didn't understand what was happening to him but, over time, an overwhelming sense of shame filled him, and it affected his life for almost four decades.

A soul dismantled

At six years old, Paul was sent away to a Christian missions boarding school, which was located far away from his home. Suddenly removed from his familiar tribal environment, he was deposited in a world he did not know. It was only then that he realized he was not a real *Dani*, but actually one of the *ghost people*. His sense of identity with the *Dani* tribe was stripped away. In one moment, he lost everything: his home, his tribe, his family, his sense of belonging. Only one dark reality remained: sexual abuse. Late at night at boarding school, the big boys came and molested the little boys.

"Nothing dismantles the human soul like sexual abuse does," Paul explains. "As children, we don't have the ability to process things like this, so we think that when things go wrong it is our fault. And as we grow up, we develop all kinds of survival mechanisms and coping skills, and we have addictions that show up inside our brokenness, because we have to have something that eases the pain and fills the emptiness."

Paul continues, "You learn from an early age that nothing and nobody is safe, so you develop all kinds of survival skills to adapt and to protect yourself."

Unfortunately, many who are broken become breakers, and so did Paul. His responses to the brokenness of his childhood included an addiction to pornography and the inability to sustain relationships. Over the years, he also learned to live behind a façade of perfectionism and performance in an attempt to hide the pain and shame of his brokenness. Pretending was also a way to silence his unanswered questions about God's apparent absence – both at that time and during his abuse as a child.

Paul wrote his best-selling book, *The Shack*, after his long and difficult healing process and now speaks of a shack as a metaphor for the human soul. "It's the house on the inside that people have helped us build, and for a lot of us it's a place where we hide our addictions and store all of our secrets," he explains. "For me, it was a place of shame, so I took large pieces of plywood and dragged them out a hundred feet around the shack of my heart and built a façade, because I didn't want anybody to come near the place of my shame and secrets and see me for who I really was."

As part of this façade, Paul based his worth on performance and winning other people's approval, which had a very destructive effect. "When you are a child, everything revolves around winning the approval and affection of those around you, and when you come from a religious background, that includes God as well," Paul explains. "You're constantly trying to figure out what people want so you can be that. And then you're told God has a whole list of things he requires of you to win *his* approval, and then everything in your life becomes performance."

The shack came crashing down

Paul became very good at performing. He went to Bible school and even worked for a church, constantly striving to win God's and people's approval. Deep within, he held on to the hope that if he could maintain a perfect performance for long enough, the fake Paul might become a real boy, a real person.

"But at some point the façades you build around you have to come down," Paul says. "I wish I could say that I finally realized

I was pretty broken and sought help, but I didn't. A lot of times when we are broken we have to get caught – and finally I was."

That happened in January of 1994, with that one-sentence phone call from his wife Kim: "I am waiting for you in your office, and I KNOW!" What Kim knew was that Paul had been involved for three months in an affair with one of her best friends.

Paul describes the confrontation: "At that point I had to make a decision whether to face Kim or kill myself. I had become a master in spinning conversations, finding excuses, and covering up escape mechanisms with religious language. But I knew that my wife's fury and her healthier black-and-white ways of seeing things wouldn't let me get away any more with being 'fifty shades of grey'."

He continues, "I don't know how, but I guess it was by the grace of God that I got to the office. Kim took me apart for four hours. Finally, I said to her, 'If we are going to face each other and work through this, I need to tell you *every secret* I have, because secrets have been killing me my whole life.'

"Naively, she said, 'Bring it on.'

"It took me the next four days to tell Kim *all* my secrets that she didn't know. She was completely shattered. When I'd finished, she said, 'I will never ever believe another word that comes out of your mouth for the rest of your life!'"

And Paul couldn't blame her. He knew he had broken her heart, her trust, and their relationship. He knew he had also broken the trust of friends and family members. But, despite the betrayals, Kim decided to let Paul continue to live in their house, because she did not want their children to grow up without a father. "And the other reason was that she knew I had hit rock bottom," Paul says. "She could tell, because I *owned* what I had done. I didn't point fingers or blame my childhood, my abuse, or other people. And I also hit rock bottom by not killing myself. Killing yourself is the last chance to run."

The shame factor

Paul had now owned all of his choices, even though he could have blamed shame for them as the underlying force that entangled him in a cobweb of hiding, breaking relationships, control, and addiction. Shame is fundamentally damaging, and, when not resolved, it leads to destructive behaviour. This was certainly true for Paul.

"One of the most profound things I discovered about shame is this: it destroys your ability to distinguish between an observation and a value statement. For instance, my wife might say, 'Paul, don't put the coloured clothes with the whites.' But what I heard was this: 'I don't know why I married such a loser of a human being as you.'"

Paul goes on, "When I married Kim, suddenly there was someone who was unknowingly poking through my thin layer of perfectionism, right through to my shame. And all I wanted to do was run away, because I was constantly interpreting everything through the lens of shame." His eventual affair, which came after years of hiding, pretending, and performing at marriage, offered him the illusion of "perfect unconditional love". However, it turned out to be a complete delusion and a total disaster.

The first step toward trust

Paul needed to get to a place where his life of lies was so exposed that it was clear to him that he had to get help. He took so long to get to that place in part because he had been abused, damaged, and hurt by the very people who should have protected him.

"I didn't trust anybody," Paul shares. "Since early childhood, trust has always been the big issue for me. I knew I had to find a way to let go of control, but control had become my default response to fear: intellectual control, conversational control, and manipulation of the people and circumstances around me."

Paul goes on, "When you hit the bottom, you stop pointing fingers. Abuse – as horrific as it is – is a prison of choice. It's the story you can go back to and then manipulate the people around you, whether consciously or unconsciously. But at some point, you have to own what you've done – and owning is huge. And I think a lot of people don't get to the point where they own it. Instead, they get sucked into something else that will give them identity, worth, value, or significance – and control does that."

After the big confrontation with Kim, one way Paul started to let go of control was by finally asking for help. "I took the yellow pages of the phone book, opened it under the heading 'Counselling', and started with A. I worked my way down till I came to the listing for Agape Youth and Family Services, which mentioned their specialization in childhood sexual abuse. I called strangers that I had never met before, and for the first time in my life I asked another human being, 'Can you help me?' And that's where I found Scott Mitchell, who became my therapist and then later my friend. That started pushing me out of my isolation toward a sense of community."

Scott Mitchell mapped out a therapy plan, then explained the stages of the process to Paul. But he warned him, "Most people bail out after a few months. Once you start feeling a bit more in control again, you'll be tempted to back out – but that's right before you hit the really tough issues." Paul agreed to the plan, determined not to back out.

The shack of personal lies

Paul gave himself fully to the therapy work he needed to do, and began the process of unravelling the lies he had believed about himself, God, and others. But several months in, he came to a place where he wanted to give up.

"When this happened, it caught me completely by surprise. I would say that was about the lowest point I experienced in my life. I was standing on the edge of an abyss and looking back at all my history, and I didn't know if one single thing about me was actually true," he says. "I didn't know what was a survival mechanism and what was actually me. I didn't know what was a façade and what was real about me. And when I hit that point, I lost all my hope." At that point, he again considered killing himself. It was only the intervention of two friends that kept him from going through with a plan to end his life.

"Dealing with what you think is the truth of your being becomes the deep issue where so much work has to be done. And it is the process of suffering that exposes the lies that underpin the way you deal with yourself, with others, and with the world," Paul explains. Healing from brokenness is possible, even from the destructiveness of sexual abuse – but it is hard work. "The whole journey was extremely tough, and for a great part it just meant slogging through another day's sense of shame, along with the fury from others – and rightly so."

Paul describes his eleven-year healing process, which led to the writing of his book, *The Shack*. It started with an intense nine-month therapy process that exposed most of the lies that had made up the prison of his soul.

"To use the metaphor of the shack, those nine months involved tearing down everything to the bare structure, right down to the foundations," Paul describes. "In that process of tearing it all down, I began to realize that so many things I had thought were true actually weren't true. That's when the lies are exposed, and that is bulldozer work. You have to go down to the bottom, into the basement and all the rooms."

The greatest risk

After the deconstruction, the slow recovery and integration

process started, and it happened primarily through the building of relationships – the very thing Paul feared the most.

"Because most of our damage happens primarily through relationships, the healing will be primarily through relationships. I'm convinced about that, because I don't think there is a truer reality about the nature and character of God than relationship," Paul emphasizes. "That's the tough part and the hard road. It's so much easier to think our way to freedom, or to take a pill. Relationships are full of mystery and full of risk, and they involve a person who is a moving target. But they are the only place where true healing and integration takes place, because trust has to be rebuilt. With help, I began to understand I had to move out of isolation and into community."

Paul clarifies that the healing process itself is different for each person. "There is no formula, as much as we would like a formula. Everybody is hurt in a different way, and the uniqueness of the damage has to do with the uniqueness of the person. That's why the presence and involvement of the Holy Spirit is so essential, because only God knows how you are crafted, and then how you were damaged, and how that needs to be healed."

The journey toward authenticity

In the past, Paul had participated in Christian counselling that had advised him to reject the past and refuse to look at what was behind. Before his façade came crumbling down, Paul tried to follow this advice, but it never brought about lasting change. Instead, it reinforced his performance. Over and over, he tried to live a "holy" life, but every time he would crash and burn. The weeds of his addictions would spring up again, because they had not been dealt with at the root.

Paul believes that true healing involves reconciliation and justice, and this only happens when the past is dealt with and the damage is healed. "I believe God is a craftsman, not a draughtsman. God has a high view of humanity," he says. "The Psalms talk about the intricacy of the human soul and the weaving of this incredible wonder. We look at the planets and we are amazed, and yet the wonders of the planets are nothing compared to a human being. But we don't look at it that way. We have a low view of humanity, so we want to *fix* it. We want to make it work without the person becoming a *real* person." He explains that we want the end product. "We want to say, 'All right. Fixed! Now I can perform in a way that is acceptable. Now I can be successful.'" However, success is something totally different from what our culture projects.

Paul describes this healing as the process of becoming an authentic human being. "All of the things that happen as a result are rather irrelevant," he says. "Success is the overflow of authenticity, or else it's not success – it's just another façade."

You cannot be authentic unless you are whole and grounded in your true identity in God. Paul summarizes it in this way: "Wholeness is when the way of your being and the truth of your being match – where your conduct and actions match who God says you are, and you agree. And that is where so much work has to be done. That is the essence of the maturing process every human being is invited to, and there is no shortcut."

Paul did not come to this realization until he dealt with his wrong religious belief systems and his understanding of who God really is. For instance, he had always read the English Bible translation of John 16:8, which says that the Holy Spirit *convicts the world of sin*. But when he studied the Greek word for "sin" in the passage, he became aware of its nuances and implied meaning.

"The word for 'sin' is *harmatia*, which means a 'negation of your origin and being'," Paul explains. "So anything that is disengaged or not integrated with your origin or being is sin – and that is brokenness, the non-authenticity. Also, the word 'convict' in the Greek language means 'expose'. So the Holy Spirit actually comes to expose what is not authentic."

The journey of authenticity is a journey of trust and turning from wrong religious beliefs to a face-to-face relationship with God. That is the essence of repenting – of re-turning to God and his truth about who we are. This involves rebuilding trust and living in the grace of one day, which is at the heart of the healing process.

But the process of getting there? Paul wouldn't wish it on his enemy. "It is so hard, because you have to challenge everything."

The shack of religious lies

For Paul, the long and slow process of unravelling the damage of the past required a major paradigm shift in his beliefs about himself and God. His religious upbringing had added another dimension to the brokenness in his soul.

"My big issue as a child was belonging. I lost all sense of belonging, and the theological doctrines I grew up with added a whole different dimension to this. I grew up with the idea that it was better to die before you messed it up. And then certain ideas of predestination and election reinforced the sense that there was no assurance of salvation. There was no sense of belonging, and that tormented my soul."

Paul was also led to believe that it was his duty to protect the mission at any cost. His parents appeared to prioritize that more highly than anything else, to the extent of "sacrificing" children on the "altar of God's purposes". And, in Paul's experience, that became linked with secrecy about the abuse he suffered.

From abuse to addiction

Paul's addiction to pornography was a result of both his experience of sexual abuse and his religious upbringing. The latter especially encouraged a detachment between head and heart.

"As soon as you do that, you create a vacuum, which needs to be filled. And one of the attractions of pornography is that the imagination of a relationship is a lot 'safer' than dealing with the potential of losses in a real one."

Paul first tried to deal with his addiction within the strictures of his religious upbringing, and within that he saw only two options. The first was self-discipline. "I was terrified of the fear of hell, and so I tried to push myself into righteous performance," he explains. "But that didn't work for long. Eventually I would crash and burn, and end up with an even greater sense of shame."

Paul's second option was to join an accountability group – but that didn't work either. "If you have an addiction, you will find a way to supply," he states.

Today, Paul says that he hasn't had an issue with addiction for twenty-two years. So what changed to enable him to conquer it? Paul started to understand his true identity in Christ, and the truth of who he is in God's sight. "I learned about the truth of my being – and the way of my being followed it. So what is the truth of my being? I'm pure of heart. That's the truth of my being. And the way I live my life flows from this truth."

The truth of your being

In order to discover his true identity, Paul had to confront the doctrines and beliefs he had grown up with.

"I had to challenge total depravity, the theology that basically teaches that all you are is a 'piece of crap', and Jesus comes and wraps you in his righteousness, so that God the

Father turns a blind eye. I had to challenge all of that by asking some fundamental questions: Was there not a good creation before I got hurt, broken, damaged, and lost? Was there not something that was whole in order for it to be broken? Can wholeness exist without brokenness? Yes. But can brokenness exist without wholeness? No. Can life exist without death? Yes. Can death exist without life? No."

As Paul learned how flawed his theology really was, he began to challenge what he believed and what he thought was certain. "This is a lot riskier, scarier, uncertain, and ambiguous, but it is also mysterious, amazing, wonderful, and life-giving, because trust always is. *Certainty and trust don't live in the same house*."

There is only one certainty, and that is the character of God. The apostle John writes, "This is the message we heard from Jesus and now declare to you: God is light, and there is no darkness in him at all" (1 John 1:5, NLT). Paul asked himself whether he believed that, and if not, why not. He found himself comparing his own desire to be a good father with his disbelief that God was a good father. He reflected that the Bible says that love doesn't keep a record of wrongs (1 Corinthians 13:5) – but it seemed that God did. "These were the beliefs I had built my world around, and everything was up for question," Paul explains.

Slowly, Paul unravelled all the lies he had believed, and the experience totally transformed his theology from a set of religious rules to a real and trusting face-to-face relationship with God. And the evidence of this paradigm shift can be seen in the way he lives.

"Now the way of my being totally matches the truth of my being. I am the same person in every situation," Paul says. "Before, it didn't matter how you lived your life. The theology was independent of the way of your being. I had a codified theology: how you lived your life was irrelevant; you just had to stick to a certain set of rules, and in the end you were never good enough anyway."

Becoming childlike

An essential part of Paul's healing process involved restoring his childlikeness and living in *the grace of today*. "I willingly had to stop 'future tripping'. We are given grace for today, but so often we miss it because we worry about things that are not real. A child naturally knows how to live in the grace of today because that's their whole universe. There is nothing beyond today, and they don't even know how to talk about two weeks ago or anything like the future. There is a wonder, a presence, and an awareness of what's going on around them that most of us don't have because we are not present," Paul shares. "It took me fifty years to become childlike and to learn to live in the simplicity of the grace of a day, to live in the here and now."

So how did he get to that point? Was it based on a single, wilful decision to trust God, as is often taught in church circles? It's not that simple.

"Real trust has to be based on real truth, and truth is a person," says Paul. "Part of the healing journey is to unmask the lies. You say that you trust because it is what you're theologically supposed to do, but as soon as something goes sideways, you are scared like everybody else. You can't truly trust someone you don't think is good. You can't truly trust someone you don't believe loves you. So when the goodness of God and the love of God are in question, then our words are nothing but empty disassociated mumbo jumbo; it's just magic."

Paul continues, "When you question that, you are masking over the lies that you actually believe about God. But God is after those lies, because they are integrated into your person, and you function out of those lies." He emphasizes that God is not impressed with religious language, because it only illustrates that the way of our being *doesn't* match the truth of our being. Its use means we don't really believe that God is good. Instead, we are creating a way of being according to some superficial definition of righteousness. Says Paul, "What we are actually doing is changing our behaviour to match what our theology says it is supposed to look like. But that's not God. That's divorcing yourself from who you are as a human being."

Paul believes that many Christians have separated the performance of their righteousness – the way of their being – from the truth of their being, because they really think they are unworthy. He explains, "If we believe theologically that the truth about us is that we are no more than a piece of crap and we are really depraved, it makes it impossible to trust God, because we are just waiting for the hammer to come down."

One of the greatest dangers of depravity theology is the disconnection between the head and the heart. Paul's healing process entailed moving from that separation to full integration. He describes it: "Finally I came to a place in my journey where I was fully integrated: I was the same person everywhere. I wasn't struggling in a hotel room all by myself, and I didn't have a world of secrets."

Of his life now, Paul says, "I am the same person in every situation. I have no secrets and I have no addictions. And I'm not talking only about being 'fifty shades of grey'. I am talking about 'gold-chain addictions', such as doing something great for God, having a platform, achieving a destiny, experiencing the anointing, or any of the empty theological words that people then make into expectations of performance."

The writing of *The Shack*

Paul's wife Kim went through her own healing process and, as Paul dealt with the lies and shared every part of the journey with her, her trust in him was slowly rebuilt. It took a long time for their relationship to heal, but after eleven years Kim came to the point where she could say that the hard work had been worth it. She then kept asking Paul to write down his experiences for their children, so he could share with them the change that had taken place in how he saw God, himself, and the world.

Then, in 2004, they experienced financial ruin. In a matter of months, they lost all their material possessions: his work, their house, their car. Yet they saw this as an opportunity to practice living in the grace for today and trusting God to provide the next meal.

Paul describes the experience: "There is nothing like losing everything to heal you from the fear of financial insecurity. Initially it was incredibly difficult, but in retrospect it became one of the most precious times in our lives, because the joy of God became our constant companion!" He continues, "That's what happens when you live inside the grace of one day – you don't run away from joy. We are so geared to be 'future trippers' – where we can't trust, where we create imaginations that don't exist, and we miss the grace that was given to us for today. By this time, I had stopped being a future tripper. I had learned to be childlike and to trust God to provide what I need one day at a time."

During that time, Paul had only two prayers left. One was this: "Papa, I don't want to be an old man one day looking back at my life, wondering, 'What would it have been like to take the risk of actually trusting?' I don't want to be that guy." His second: "Papa, I'm never again going to ask you to bless anything I do. I'm done with performance, achievement, and trying to make things happen. But if you have something you want to bless, and it would be okay for me to be part of that, I'll be all over it – and I don't care if that is cleaning toilets, holding a door open for someone, or whatever. I just want to know at the end of the day that *you did this and I got to participate!*"

Paul had three jobs: cleaning offices, handling shipping and receiving, and working as a hotel night clerk. On his commute on the train between work and the outskirts of Portland he began to write a story to give to his six children for Christmas. After all, he didn't have any money to buy gifts, so a story of his own making it would be. When Kim had asked him to write something for their children, she had been hoping for six to eight pages – but when Paul was done, he had completed a fascinating novel of 250 pages: *The Shack*.

The story starts with a mysterious note Mackenzie Allen Phillips (Mack) receives one day in his mailbox. Four years earlier, Mack's youngest daughter Missy was abducted during a family vacation and brutally murdered by a serial killer. Her blood-stained clothes were found in an abandoned shack deep in the Oregon wilderness, but her body has never been found. Since that time, Mack has been haunted by a *great sadness*. Then one day he receives a note from "Papa", the name his wife uses for God, inviting Mack to return to the same shack. Uncertain of what to expect, Mack goes to the place of his greatest devastation, where he experiences a weekend-long encounter with the Godhead. Papa, or God the Father, appears in the form of a large African American woman named Elousia (the Creator and Ground of all Being), Jesus is a middle-aged man of Middle-Eastern descent, and the Holy Spirit is revealed as an Asian woman called Sarayu. Each in turn engages Mack in conversation and leads him to the places of pain in his heart, slowly transforming them as Mack lets go of the lies, wrong paradigms, and resentments.

Paul made fifteen spiral-bound copies of his story at Office Depot in time to give them to his children for Christmas. It was never his intention to publish the story. But he gave a few of the copies to his friends and family, who in turn shared copies with other friends. From there, the story started spreading like wildfire.

Three acquaintances approached Paul and encouraged him to publish the book, with the long-term goal of one day making a film. The four of them sought a publishing agreement, but *The Shack* was rejected by twenty-six different publishers. Christian publishers considered the story too edgy and risky. Secular publishers liked the story, but said there was "too much Jesus" in it. So two of them created Windblown Media and self-published the book in 2007. Selling books out of a garage, two storage units, and the local printer in Los Angeles, and with no marketing other than a simple website and word-of-mouth referrals, they sold more than one million copies in thirteen months.

The Shack is a phenomenon that nobody saw coming. It gave people a new language with which to have a conversation about God that was relational and not religious. It broke down walls and reached the precious places of people's hearts.

"The story of *The Shack* is absolutely crazy," Paul says today. "God totally surprised everyone. In retrospect, I see God saying with his sense of humour, 'Hey Paul, you know this book you're writing for your kids for Christmas? What if I bless that? You give it to your kids, and then I'll give it to mine.'"

The Shack sold more than twenty million copies worldwide and is among the top 100 best-selling fiction books in all of history. In March 2017, it was released as a top-notch Hollywood film by Lionsgate, starring Octavia Spencer (Papa), Sam Worthington (Mack), and Aviv Alush, who was the first Jewish actor in history to portray Jesus in a major film.

That's how crazy the story is.

Paul's journey toward healing has been an excruciatingly painful and intense process, but in the end it was worth it; not because of the outward success, but because of the inward.

Chapter Nine
Wounded Healers

Choosing forgiveness and reconciliation
Desmond Tutu

God, I know you are in charge; I just wish you would
make it slightly more obvious!
Desmond Tutu, Archbishop Emeritus of Cape Town

They had been driving for hours in the scorching heat
along the vast endless plains of the Karoo desert, and the
children had started nagging and bickering in the back seat
of their station wagon.

"This heat is killing me," Desmond mumbled, and then
jerked his head toward his children. "Stop fighting! For
goodness' sake, this is driving me crazy!" He was on edge, and
so was everyone else.

The youngest two, Naomi and Mpho, started crying. "We're
so hot! Can't we stop? This always takes so long!"

They hadn't even managed half of the sixteen-hour trip
from the Eastern Cape up to Krugersdorp near Johannesburg,
where they would spend the night with Desmond's parents.
The next day, they would complete the last five-hour stretch to
Swaziland.

"We'll take a break soon," Desmond's wife Leah tried to
calm the children. But, in reality, they would have to press
on. There were no hotels or inns on the way that would
accommodate blacks at any price.

"Apartheid was active at full force,"[1] Tutu writes in *The Book of Forgiving*. "And that was the reason for their trip.

Several years before, in 1953, the apartheid government of South Africa had instituted the Bantu Education Act, which introduced a racially segregated education system. Enforcing an inferior education for blacks, it essentially relegated them to manual labour. Desmond and Leah had both left the teaching profession in protest, and they had vowed never to subject their children to this arrangement. The only way to bypass Bantu education was to send their children to boarding school in the neighbouring country of Swaziland.

Mirage vs oasis

The trip was always a drag. Aside from fatigue and the unbearable heat, the anticipation of their impending separation for the next boarding-school term added another level of peevishness to the atmosphere in the car. Trevor and Theresa, the two eldest seated by the doors, rolled down the windows in the hope of catching a breeze, but the desert wind was like the scorching air that rushes out when opening an oven.

They were just reaching a remote desert town when Desmond's eyes lit up at the sight of an oasis in the endless desert drive: a sign on the side of the road that read "Wall's Ice Cream". That was exactly what they needed! He pointed out the sign, and immediately the mood in the car lifted. Desmond could almost feel the cold creaminess refreshing his scorched throat as they pulled into the driveway. He stumbled out of the car and walked up to the door.

Desmond had hardly entered the store when the boy standing behind the register stabbed his hand in the air, pointing to the window and yelling, "*Kaffir!* Read the sign!"[2]

Desmond looked at the window and, as he recounts in his book, he read, "No black man's feet allowed on the hallowed ground of this store"[3] – except probably for scrubbing the toilets and floors.

That was it! The pain of the impending separation from the children, their whining, the heat, the fatigue – and now this! Anger flared up inside him, and he rushed out and told everyone, "Get back in the car!" The children were confused but could sense the trouble brewing in the air. No one said a word.

"I was furious," Desmond writes. "And like so many frustrated parents, my temper flared. Underneath my temper, however, was a bright, burning wound."[4]

Second-class citizens

Even though this had been a less significant instance of discrimination, with no physical injuries, the hurt was very deep.

"It was a stinging hurt that was heaped on all the other hurts that were commonplace in our daily lives under apartheid. We were so used to these incidents that, at the time, I didn't consciously realize I had to forgive the boy behind the register,"[5] Desmond relates in his book.

Desmond Tutu's life is a story of numerous personal assaults, obstacles, and hardships, all stemming from the time of his struggle against the apartheid regime. In a similar way to Nelson Mandela, he also had to take a long walk to freedom. One of the world's most famous priests, he was awarded the Nobel Peace Prize in 1984 for his relentless efforts to speak up for the oppressed and to fight injustice. As a black man in South Africa, the injustices he himself suffered were manifold. He was beaten, handcuffed, ridiculed, and received many death threats, but these assaults were not the worst apartheid had to offer.

"Growing up under the apartheid regime had such a tremendous effect on how you saw yourself as a human being," Tutu disclosed in our interview. "You always felt you were a second-class citizen, that you were not quite as 'human' as the others – the whites. The apartheid ideology affected our way of thinking and we were often deeply humiliated by all the segregation laws."

He continued, "We had separate entrances for blacks and whites to go into the bank or the post office, and we had separate exits – but then we all used the same street. It was ridiculous!"

The unforgivable offence

Tutu shared one such experience that occurred after the Tutu family had just returned to South Africa from England. For four years, while Desmond completed his Masters in Theology at King's College in London, they lived in England, and their youngest daughter Mpho was born there. Tutu was then called back to South Africa to be the Anglican Dean of St Mary's Cathedral in Johannesburg.

One Sunday afternoon back in South Africa, the Tutus were outside with their children when little Mpho saw some white children playing on swings at a playground. "I want to go there and play too," she said.

But Desmond had to tell her, "No, sweetheart, you can't."

Mpho didn't understand. "But why?" she demanded "There are other children playing over there!"

"That was so difficult," Desmond related in our conversation. "I just wanted the ground to open and swallow me up. How did I tell my child, 'Yes, you are a child, but you are not a child like these other children on the swings and roundabouts'?" He continued, "Instances like these were the most difficult. How apartheid affects you as a grown-up is one thing, but, as a parent, how it affects your child is a totally different thing, and there was nothing you could do about it! That was the worst aspect of apartheid, because it made you feel so helpless."

Tutu willingly tolerated intimidation, death threats, and discrimination. But it really gutted him when it involved his family. In an interview with Norwegian journalist Fredrik Skavlan, he shared: "One thing I found almost unforgivable was when the people who tried to threaten me would call our house, and one of my children would pick up the phone. I should think they would say, 'Go get your father or mother.' But instead they would say to my children, 'Tell your father we are going to kill him!' I could see the anxious look on their face after they hung up the phone, and it made me really angry. I chose this work to fight against apartheid; my children didn't."

Another time, Tutu's wife Leah was handcuffed and paraded through the streets of Johannesburg for a minor traffic offence. "And that really made me furious; it took long to forgive that type of offence."[6]

No future without forgiveness

In an interview with broadcast journalist David Frost, Tutu disclosed that in the early stages of the struggle against apartheid, he experienced anger toward God. "I would often say, 'God, I know you are in charge; I just wish you would make it slightly more obvious!' I didn't doubt God, I never have, but when things in our nation didn't improve, I sometimes got really angry at him. I would rail at him and say, 'For goodness' sake! Why don't you do something about this!'"[7]

With time, though, he learned that there is only one way forward, and that is the path of forgiveness.

"What I learned throughout my life is that there is no future without forgiveness," Tutu reiterated in our conversation. "I often would repeat the saying, 'There go I but for the grace of God.' I was constantly reminding myself that if I had been exposed to the same pressures, circumstances, and conditions as the particular person who humiliated me or insulted my pride, could I be sure that I would not have done the same and turned out the same way? No, I couldn't. I hope I would not have, but I couldn't be sure that I would not have turned out to be an oppressor."

Tutu's core message to the nation of South Africa and to the world has been that there is no future without forgiveness. He served in a vital role as the chair of the nation's Truth and Reconciliation Commission (TRC), facilitating the process of forgiveness and reconciliation in the aftermath of the abolition of apartheid.

But before going deeper into Tutu's insights on the process of how forgiveness is possible, even for the most ghastly atrocities, let's first have a look at his early life, how his main message developed, and how he became one of the world's most famous priests.

Escaping death

Tutu's career was not a stellar one, planned out or pursued in detail. On the contrary, it was all rather accidental. Desmond Tutu never aspired to become a priest, although one of his main mentors and role models in his early life was a priest. Tutu says about his own life that God "forced" him into his destiny.[8] This becomes clearer when you compare what he had originally planned for his life with what he ultimately became.

Desmond Tutu was born in 1931 in Klerksdorp, an impoverished township on the outskirts of Johannesburg. He was a frail and sickly baby, and his parents feared he would not survive and would end up like his older brother, who had died before Desmond was born. To everyone's surprise he did survive, and his grandmother then gave him the middle name Mpilo, which means "life". Desmond was a very cheerful child and was loved for his great sense of humour. He was a peace lover and as such had a mild and non-confrontational temperament.[9] This would prove to be one of the greatest challenges for him to overcome later when he had to take on the leadership role in the nation's struggle against the white apartheid regime.

"My greatest weakness was being scared!" Tutu professed in our conversation. The whites hated him because he was speaking up for the oppressed, but the blacks opposed him, too, because he preached non-violent resistance. Caught up in the heat of the conflict, he received criticism and attack from both sides.

From his early childhood, Desmond carried within him a strong sense of justice. This may have stemmed from his experience of his father's repeated drunken and violent outbursts at home. When his father was drunk, he would beat Desmond's mother. As a boy, Desmond felt a strong resentment toward him.

"I wanted to protect my mother and beat him up, but I was too small," Desmond recalled. "My father was a great man in many respects, but when he got drunk, he was awful. I wanted to hurt him like he had hurt my mother. As a boy, I was very angry with him, and it wounded my soul. Even after I had worked through a long process of forgiveness, I still carried some residue of anger and pain when I thought back to those times."

Desmond's mother was the most important person in his life, and one of the people who shaped him the most.

"I resemble my mother physically. I got my big nose from her, which I have to put into everything," Tutu chuckled. "She was short and stumpy and had a big nose like I do, and I have often prayed that I might not only resemble her physically, but also in her love and compassion for others. Although she was not educated, she was an incredible human being, and she had a huge influence on my life."

Small token with lasting impact

Tutu vividly remembers an incident with his mother that made a deep and lasting impression on him.

"I was about nine years old, and my mother was working at a school for the blind as a domestic worker. She took me along one day, and I saw a white priest approaching. When he passed by, he tipped his hat and said, 'Madam,' greeting my mother. I was stunned. I had never seen a white person greet my mother in respect, let alone call her *madam!*"

Just a few years later, at the age of fourteen, Desmond was diagnosed with tuberculosis (TB). He had always been thin and frail, but this was the most serious illness of his life, and when he started coughing up blood, the doctors feared he would not survive. He ended up spending long months in sterile hospital surroundings, which he found extremely difficult. He experienced intense feelings of isolation, loneliness, and despair during his twenty-month treatment away from home.[10]

During this time, the same priest he had encountered years before made a major impact on Desmond, which would stay with him for the rest of his life. In our conversation he remembered, "I was hospitalized for nearly two years, and this priest visited me every week. If he couldn't, then he sent a member of his community to visit me. Even though I didn't know at the time that I was learning, I learned from him how you can make someone feel important. There was this important white person visiting me – a black child, a 'non-entity' in South Africa – every week and paying so much attention to me! This did something incredible for my self-esteem."

The priest, named Trevor Huddleston, demonstrated love in action, and he also taught Desmond another very important lesson: that not all white people were the same. Trevor Huddleston would become Desmond's mentor, and later an important anti-apartheid figure in Britain.

During Desmond's long hospitalization, Huddleston provided him with many books, which he eagerly devoured in order to pass his school exams. During that time, Desmond developed a great love for literature and became an avid reader. During Huddleston's many visits to Desmond's room, he also discussed South Africa's problems with him openly.

As a result of the inspiring example of Father Huddleston, Desmond's faith deepened greatly during his time in hospital.[11] He also thrived academically. The TB rendered his right hand partially paralyzed, so he taught himself to write left-handed. Despite his long absence from school, he passed the Joint Matriculation Board Exams in 1950 and was among the 0.5 per cent of black Africans who qualified for university entrance.

Detour or destiny?

Desmond's father hoped he would follow in his footsteps and go into teaching, but Desmond's dream was to become a medical doctor. He had developed a love for medicine while in hospital, and he had a specific interest in researching TB, which had so devastated his own health. In addition, Desmond aspired to become one of the few black Africans to achieve high academic and professional goals. There was only one Western-trained black African doctor in the nation, who practiced medicine in Sophiatown, and Tutu was inspired by his example.

Desmond was admitted to medical school at the University of the Witwatersrand in Johannesburg, but, to his great dismay, he was unable to raise the tuition fees for this elite institution. Eventually, he was forced to make other plans. Career options for blacks were limited, and the most obvious choice was to become a teacher, so that was what he did. Unfortunately, that only lasted until his resignation in protest of the Bantu Education Act. The only remaining viable option for black South Africans with academic aspirations was to pursue a career in the church.

At the age of twenty-nine, Desmond started all over again and began his training to become an Anglican priest at St Peter's Theological College in Johannesburg in 1958. Even though the priesthood was not what he had in mind initially, it was there that he found his real passion and call in life. Of course, he had no idea of the path that would open up before him: to become possibly the world's most famous priest and God's megaphone in the struggle for human rights and justice in South Africa.

Passion for compassion

By the time Tutu started retraining in the church, he and Leah were married and their first two children, Trevor and Theresa, had been born. Leah had also left the teaching profession and retrained as a nurse. Starting over demanded a lot of sacrifices from them both. But they stayed true to themselves and did not shy away from discomfort or inconvenience in order to stand up for what they believed.

The problems of apartheid not only permeated the school system, but also seeped through the infrastructure of the church. Black African ministers faced lower pay and fewer options for advancement in the white-controlled church. For example, the scholarship that Tutu received for training as a priest was lower than the standard amount designated for whites. White curates were provided with housing, but when Desmond was ordained as a curate, he and Leah, together with their three children, had to live in a garage on the outskirts of the township of their assigned parish. That garage was their main bedroom, the children's bedroom, their lounge, and dining room all rolled into one.[12]

Despite the difficult conditions, Tutu undertook his duties as clergyman very diligently. He visited his parishioners regularly in their even poorer township homes and listened to their concerns, their pains, and their questions. In ministering to the overwhelmingly poor members of his congregation, Tutu developed a deep compassion and an intense passion for the priesthood. Soon after he was ordained as a priest in 1961, new doors opened for him to increase his qualifications in England by studying for a Master's degree in theology.

Dignity restored

Tutu's time in Britain was not only an important stepping stone that eventually led him on to an international platform in the fight for justice in South Africa. It was also a time of personal reshaping and internal preparation for this future task. Desmond and Leah were astounded by their newfound freedom in Britain. It had a deep impact on him, developing his confidence and helping him shed the deeply ingrained sense of racial inferiority. Both of them enjoyed the liberty they experienced in Britain. Desmond especially made a game of hearing people address him with respect.

"When we saw a policeman we would stop him and ask him for directions, even if we knew where we were going!" Tutu told us. "We did it for the mere pleasure of being called *sir* or *madam* – something that was just unthinkable in South Africa! There we would have been asked for our passes and ran the risk of being arrested."

This liberating experience helped him to become, as he has described it, "more fully human", and slowly freed him from his sense of inferiority as a black man.[13]

During Tutu's time in Britain between 1962 and 1966, he led a parish that included white parishioners. Again, this new experience helped him overcome the habit of automatically deferring to whites. He developed the confidence to disagree openly with whites, and he felt freer to express his opinions than he had ever been able to in South Africa.

"It was very liberating not to experience daily discrimination, and it was there that I actually realized how deeply apartheid had affected me," Tutu remembered.

In another interview, he related, "You know the worst thing about apartheid was how it made you feel about yourself, the way it made you doubt that you were actually really a child of God. When you are constantly subjected to discrimination, it begins to work on your mind. You start thinking, 'Maybe they are right. Maybe I am just a second-class human being. Maybe I am of lesser value.'"[14]

Tutu went on to describe how he discovered the power of language and what it can do to a person. "Language does not just describe reality. Language *creates* the reality it describes. So when you are called a *non-European*, a *non-this* or a *non-that*, you might think it does not affect you, but it is in fact very corrosive to your self-image. You end up wondering whether you are actually as human as these others."[15]

Desmond's experience in Britain helped him to overcome the effects the apartheid labelling had had on his feelings about himself. Then, when back in South Africa, he recognized more and more how this sense of inferiority among black South Africans actually dehumanized them and caused them to treat each other poorly. He also began to believe that an important part in healing the nation would be the restoration of a sense of personal dignity.

Looking the beast in the eye

But even in Tutu's own life, the apartheid ideology had a lasting impact on his thinking, catching him by surprise when it surfaced. In our conversation, he described one such instance: "One time I boarded a plane in Nigeria and then saw that both the pilot and co-pilot were black. And you know what happened? A sudden feeling of unease crept into my consciousness. I was wondering whether these two black pilots were actually capable of flying this plane!" After take-off, the flight got a bit bumpy. "I was holding on to my seat, sweating and wondering whether we'd make it!" Tutu laughed as he painted the picture for us. Of course, he arrived at his destination safely. "It was instances like these, but in particular during the hearings of the Truth and Reconciliation Commission, that we had to realize we were deeply wounded people."

How do you heal a people that have been crushed under the oppression of such a dehumanizing system as apartheid? How South Africa functioned in the years after apartheid was abolished is still considered a miracle, because everyone had expected the nation to erupt into a bloodbath of retaliation. But, for South Africa's new leaders, the recent events in Rwanda had been a daunting warning sign. They knew that they had to deal with their past in a different way if they wanted to avoid a similar situation.

"You have to look the beast in the eye," Tutu insisted in a speech on truth and reconciliation. "Forgetting the past is not an option! That's what we learned from Rwanda. It reminds me of the haunting inscription at the entrance of the Dachau concentration camp museum: 'Those who forget the past are doomed to repeat it.' The past dealt with by silencing it does not remain the past. It refuses to lie down quietly," he continued. "Bygones don't become bygones just by your say-so. You cannot just say, 'Be gone!' Bygones will return to haunt you – and we had just witnessed this in Rwanda: the Tutsis had done something to the Hutus a long time ago, and it seemed to be gone. But after thirty years the ghost from the past returned and the Hutus struck back with relentless rage and revenge."[16]

The importance of truth

Tutu explains that when you try to silence the past, you actually re-victimize the victim. "When you say, 'Let's forget about it,' you are in essence saying to the victims that what happened in their case either didn't happen or that it doesn't matter. And that is very detrimental. So we had to ask ourselves how we were going to deal with our past, and we chose a compromise: we offered amnesty to the perpetrators in exchange for truth."[17]

When Nelson Mandela became President of South Africa in 1994 and asked Desmond Tutu to chair the nation's Truth and Reconciliation Commission to deal with the atrocities that had been committed under apartheid, Tutu knew that the task ahead was daunting. In fact, the decision was met with scepticism at first, and the leaders were accused of letting people get away with murder. But as the process continued, many came to see the wisdom in it.

Tutu recounts, "Sometimes victims were heard for the first time when they shared their story of personal suffering, and we have found that just in *telling the story*, people experienced a catharsis, a healing." Tutu compared the TRC's task with that of opening a wound and cleansing it, so that in the end the country could be healed.

In total, the TRC listened to more than 20,000 individual testimonies about the ghastly acts that had been committed during apartheid. And Tutu insisted on hearing the stories of the "little people", not just the big stories that had already been told. He wanted to hear from the people in little towns in faraway places, whose suffering had been ignored for so long.

During the very first hearing of the TRC, Tutu broke down crying. "It was terrible, because I cry easily," he says. He immediately recognized that he couldn't allow that to happen again, because: "The media then concentrated on me, instead of the people who were the rightful subjects of attention. After that first hearing I was determined that if I was going to cry, I would cry at home or at church – and that's what I did."[18] During subsequent hearings, Tutu would often bite his own hand when he began to feel emotional, in order not to divert the focus from the victims.

Many of the victims' testimonies heard by the TRC were absolutely horrendous and heartbreaking.

"We are talking about rape, torture, and genocide. We thought there was no end to the cruelty and ghastly atrocities people can come up with and were willing to do to other people," Tutu reported in the online documentary 'Apartheid, Perpetrators, Forgiveness'.[19]

What sustained Tutu during this time – and, in fact, throughout his whole life – was prayer. He says, "There are so many noises around us, and I personally need to seek the quiet to hear God and commune with him. I was trained as a priest in a convent, and I stuck to the regimen of early devotion. So that is something I have practiced ever since I became a priest, and it has sustained me throughout all the years."

He continues, "And then there are the prayers of so many others, which have sustained me. Without the prayers that so many have offered for me, I could not have made it."

Becoming wounded healers

Even though the TRC was a political council and not a religious one, Tutu led them in prayer before each hearing, asking the Holy Spirit to bring comfort and healing to the nation. Besides revealing and acknowledging the horrible suffering of the victims, the Commission also provided the perpetrators with opportunities to make amends.

Tutu recounted in one television interview: "Most of them were actually quite genuine when they asked for forgiveness from the victims. They were not required to do that, yet many of them did. And it was an incredible privilege to have been part of the whole process, to be wounded healers. We realized this more and more during this period of the hearings of the

TRC, that we are a wounded people, and that we are wounded healers."[20]

Contrary to what many expected, what is most remembered and valued from the TRC process is not the revelation of the ghastly acts and atrocities that were committed, but rather the incredible generosity and magnanimity of the many victims who forgave. One nineteen-year-old girl named Babalwa spoke about the grief and hardship her family experienced after her father was killed by the apartheid regime. Only eight at the time, she was left to raise her three-year-old brother.

"I would love to know who killed my father. So would my brother," Babalwa said when she shared her heartbreaking story before the TRC. But what she said next astonished everyone. "We want to know, because we want to forgive – but we don't know *who* to forgive."[21]

Understanding forgiveness

How is such forgiveness possible? The TRC heard many extraordinary stories of forgiveness, but Tutu insisted (in a different interview) that we all have the capacity to be extraordinary. "We might think we wouldn't be able to do that when we hear these testimonies. But you don't know. You don't know how you really would react. The *capacity to forgive* is in each one of us, but it is something you actually do for yourself. By forgiving you serve your peace of mind and spirit. Forgiveness serves your own well-being. When you are wronged, humiliated, or hurt, your blood pressure goes up and you feel it in your tumtum. But when you forgive, your blood pressure goes down, and you are able to release anger and hatred. So forgiveness is good for your physical and your spiritual well-being. It is what you do for your own sake."[22]

In the previously mentioned documentary on forgiveness, Tutu explained that you find freedom for yourself in the act of forgiving. "The person who has done the evil deed will face consequences, but until you are willing to forgive them, you are still tied to them. You continue to be punished by what they have done."

Tutu goes on to explain how to break the vicious cycle of unforgiveness. "By the fact that someone has wronged, hurt, or abused us, we have a certain right over that person in that we could refuse to forgive. We could keep the right to retribution. But when I forgive, I jettison that right and I open the door of opportunity for the other person to make a new beginning. That is what I do when I forgive."[23]

The victims in South Africa experienced acts of cruelty and torture. Is it possible that these can be forgiven, and can real reconciliation actually occur between the victim and this kind of perpetrator?

Tutu shares his answer: "Well, as a Christian, I have to ask: is there anything that is unforgivable? I'm afraid we are following a Lord and Master who, at the point where he was tortured and crucified in the most painful way, prayed for those who tortured him, and he even found an excuse for them: 'They do not know what they are doing.' And we follow one who says, 'Forgive one another as God in Christ forgave you.' That is for us the paradigm. We might not always reach that ideal, but that is the standard."[24]

The path of forgiveness is not an easy one, and, depending on the severity of the harm caused, it can be a long walk to find the freedom that is released in forgiveness. Tutu does not make light of the cost of this process. "On this path we must walk through the muddy shoals of hatred and anger and make our way through grief and loss to find the acceptance that is the hallmark of forgiveness."[25] It would be easier if there were clear steps to follow, and if the path of forgiveness was clearly marked out, but it is not. For some, granting forgiveness may happen quickly, maybe even within seconds. For others, it may take months or even years, depending on the severity of the harm.

Granting forgiveness can also be more difficult when the perpetrator does not show any remorse. "Of course, it is preferable if the perpetrator asks for forgiveness," Tutu states. But in the end, the path of forgiveness is the only path worth following, and the only way forward into healing.

Forgiveness is not easy

Some people, even some in Christian communities, have unknowingly adopted a Buddhist concept of forgiveness, believing that forgiveness entails letting go of the sorrow and dying to the past. But Desmond Tutu corrects this misconception in the documentary. "I doubt that you are able by an act of will to let go of the pain. The *will* part of forgiveness is where you say, 'I am not going to let you victimize me and hold me in a position where I harbour resentment against you, and where I am looking for an opportunity to pay you back. I am letting go of that right.'"[26] In other words, forgiving does not mean forgetting the harm. Neither does it mean pretending that the injury was not as bad as it really was. "Quite the opposite is true," Tutu states in his book. "The cycle of forgiveness can be activated and completed only with absolute truth and honesty."[27]

That's why the TRC only granted amnesty to the perpetrators in exchange for the *truth*. It's also the reason why they made a point of listening to the thousands of individual victims' testimonies of personal suffering. "What we found is that people seemed to find a great deal of healing just in being able to tell their story. I suppose in some way it was authenticating them," Tutu says. "And by listening to their story, it was as if we were saying 'We acknowledge that you are you, and that you are someone of infinite worth and value.'"[28]

The most important lesson that Tutu takes away from the TRC process is that no situation is completely beyond redemption. He describes it in the forgiveness documentary:

"We all learned that there is no situation of which we can say, 'This is absolutely, totally devoid of hope,' because that is what people thought about South Africa."[29]

He also reveals his belief that the real heroes of the Commission's work were those who might be called "ordinary people": "There are no ordinary people in my theology, but it is the small people, the ones who used to be non-entities, that are the stars. It's been an incredible privilege to listen to people who rightfully should have been consumed by anger, bitterness, and revenge. When you experience their magnanimity, their willingness to forgive, it actually shows how incredibly good and generous these people are. It is not just fiction when we say we are made in the image of God – we are made for goodness. That is so incredible!"[30]

Prisoner of hope

Desmond Tutu believes that this capacity for good exists at the heart of every individual. For this he is often called an optimist. But he refutes that: "I'm not an optimist; I'm simply a prisoner of hope. When we understand God's dream and calling on our lives, we can only be amazed! We are created in the image of God! Even the person who has done the evil deed is created in the image of God. We are, in fact, God-carriers!" However, he acknowledges, "We don't really believe this. We dismiss people who don't fit into our mould – the criminal, the beggar on the street."

Tutu is passionate in his belief that all humans are God-carriers. "If we had the right kind of eyes we would see God there! God doesn't just say 'I love you' when you are likable. He says 'I love you' even when people see you at your worst!"[31]

Tutu illustrates this idea in another interview, using the Bible story of the good shepherd. "Most churches show us a picture of a shepherd with a lamb. But lambs don't stray; it's the grown-up sheep that stray. The sheep that strayed was a troublesome old ram – and that's what the shepherd went after, leaving the good sheep behind! God turns our kinds of values upside down, because I would generally invest in someone who is good. But God says, 'I will invest in one they say is bad,' because he knows their true identity and what they are made of! He knows their potential, their calling to be God-carriers, and he calls them back."[32]

Dream dreams

Because Desmond sees this potential for goodness in people, his greatest advice is to dream dreams.

"Don't be infected by the cynicism in this world. God wants to use you. Believe that this world can become a better place, a world where there is room for everyone, a world where you have the capacity to include all and not be shaken and scared by the successes of others!"

He continues, "Dream of a world where poverty is history, where everyone knows they have a place in God's heart. Young people dream dreams, but then they grow up and forget them. Don't forget your dreams! Dream!"

Desmond Tutu is a truly humble person and a carrier of hope. His joy is contagious and, at the age of eighty-five, his wit and sense of humour have not diminished. When I asked him in our interview if he would do anything differently if he could live his life again, he said impishly, "Become an adult!" and laughed heartily. But the reality is that he is an icon who has learned to keep his childlikeness while taking on immense responsibility. Despite all the challenges, struggles, and obstacles he has faced, he celebrates life. Although some of Tutu's liberal views have not been without controversy, his theology of forgiveness and transformation leaves a legacy of hope.

Tutu also focuses on the individual and truly knows how to make someone feel important. His character, compassion, integrity, and authenticity have made him an example for his people. And his message that there is no future without forgiveness motivated a whole nation to engage in a process of forgiveness and reconciliation.

But what is at the root of his convictions? His own experience of forgiveness. He himself was wounded – in childhood by an alcoholic parent, during his teenage years in his battle with TB, by the unrealized dream of becoming a doctor. That was in addition to the racial oppression, personal assaults, and death threats he experienced under apartheid. But a personal journey through the process of forgiveness has transformed him.

We learn from Tutu that no situation is totally devoid of hope. Whatever challenge, pain, loss, betrayal, grief, or obstacle you have experienced, if you walk on the path of forgiveness and reconciliation, your situation can be transformed. What was lost can be restored and redeemed in ways you cannot imagine when you take the journey to heal the wounds of the past, and you yourself become a wounded healer.

Chapter Ten
Greatness in the Making

*Understanding the process
of transformation*

Dear child of God,
I'm sorry to say that suffering is not optional.
Suffering is part and parcel of the human condition,
but suffering can either embitter or ennoble us.
It can ennoble us and become a spirituality of
transformation when we find meaning in it.

Desmond Tutu

When Nelson Mandela became President of South Africa in 1994, one of the first people he invited to the statehouse was the man who had been the prosecutor in his trial for treason twenty-seven years earlier – the man who had sent him to Robben Island and had actually argued for his death sentence! Later, he invited the widows of former political leaders who had persecuted him to dine with him. And he even undertook a long journey to visit the widow of former apartheid legislator Dr Hendrik Verwoerd – the man who had engineered and implemented the racial policies of apartheid.

Desmond Tutu still marvels at Mandela's actions. "For someone who had been the commander in chief of the military wing of the ANC to be at the forefront of persuading our people to lay down their arms and then to actually live this out, is incredible! He even invited his white jailer to his inauguration ceremony! If we hadn't had someone of the stature like Mandela [doing this], it would have been very difficult to convince people in his ranks to lay down their arms."[1]

Nelson Mandela's contribution to South Africa's peaceful transformation into a free nation is immeasurable. But Tutu reminds us that Mandela was not always so magnanimous. "Many people say that the twenty-seven years Mandela was imprisoned were such a waste of his life, that he could have accomplished so much more, but I tell them that it was not a waste." He explains further: "People don't understand that heroes don't fall from heaven; they are formed on earth. When Mandela first got to Robben Island he was an angry young man."[2]

Mandela's years of physical confinement contributed to the internal transformation process that would lead him into true freedom and turn him into the great man who emerged from prison. The very years that seemed like a waste, that appeared to take him further away from the realization of his dream of a free South Africa, actually turned out to be his most crucial formative years, preparing him to lead South Africa through a peaceful transition.

Understanding the process of a dream

When we catch hold of a dream – whether through a vision, clear calling, or longings and desires in our heart – our initial response is one of zeal and excitement. We want to run with it, convinced that we will see the dream fulfilled right away – as soon as tomorrow or next week. Charged up, we make plans for it to come to pass. But then something happens – and this throws many dream chasers off course. We are confronted with contradictions and obstacles that are diametrically opposed to the fulfilment of the dream. Reality suddenly doesn't look at all like what we had dreamed or imagined.

When we examine the lives of great leaders of our time, along with heroes from the Bible, a particular pattern emerges, and it is a critical preparation process on the way to fulfilling our destiny. Jacob's life as recorded in Genesis 29 shows the blueprint: Jacob had a dream – and his dream was to marry Rachel. But the morning after the wedding he woke up with Leah instead. That had not been the deal! Regardless of whether Leah was desirable or not – and the Bible is not clear on that question – she was not the woman he had dreamed of. Yet an important part of his destiny was hidden in exactly what he didn't want: in time, it was *Leah* who bore him Judah, not Rachel. And Jesus the Messiah was later born into the line of Judah, not into that of either of Rachel's sons.

Jacob laboured for another seven years under the oppression of his father-in-law after he married Rachel. But those years of betrayal, deception, injustice, and disappointments didn't just give him what he wanted. They changed his identity – literally. Jacob (a name that means "deceiver") eventually became Israel (which means "a prince with God"). An angel of the Lord told him, "Your name will no longer be Jacob. You have wrestled with God and with men, and you have prevailed" (Genesis 32:28). Interestingly, the Hebrew word for prevail means "overcome, suffer or endure".[3] Jacob's path to his destiny was riddled with contradictions. But he persevered and eventually got past them. Similar patterns of contradiction and opposition occurred in the lives of Joseph, Moses, and David – to name just a few.

Unfortunately, when God gives us one dream, and we wake up to another reality (Leah) – one that does not look as "beautiful" as we anticipated – we are often surprised. We tend to think that contradictions and disappointments are not supposed to happen in our walk with God. When faced with them, we wonder if it means we have made a major mistake. Sometimes we even become disillusioned and give up. An overemphasis on prosperity and breakthrough in the

Western church has reinforced this concept. But if we realize that the process of preparation will actually help us to sustain the dream in the long run, and if we understand that God's plans and purposes are greater than our dream, we can lean into the process of transformation and cooperate with what God is doing.

When God gives us a dream, he works first on expanding the internal capacity of our hearts to carry the full manifestation of the dream. Premature attempts to fulfil it on our own terms usually expose our immaturity and end in disaster. Mandela's early attempts to bring about a free South Africa included guerrilla warfare; Moses' first attempt to bring justice and freedom to his people involved murder; Joseph's first attempt to take the lead over his brothers demonstrated arrogance and pride. In all cases, God had a different plan to bring about the dream and freedom they were longing for, and it turned out to be a much better way.

Getting over ourselves

Floyd McClung said in one of his sermons, "Between the mountain of promise (or dream) and the mountain of fulfilment is the valley of testing." If it were up to us, we would jump from mountaintop to mountaintop. But the only way to get to the mountaintop of the fulfilment of the dream is through the valley, which prepares us to carry God's promise and dream to full term. It does this in two ways. First, the valley of testing develops strength of character in our lives. Second, it is also a "valley of the shadow of death". In other words, it is where things that hinder the full manifestation of God's dream need to die. In Mandela's case, what needed to die was anger, which – if he had continued to pursue that path – would have precipitated civil war. Moses' temper also got the better of him, and it needed to die before it caused more bloodshed. In Joseph's case, what needed to die was pride and arrogance, which would have resulted in humiliation and oppression.

The specific things that need to die in that valley are different for every person. But there is one thing that needs to die in all of our lives: our own selves. To fulfil God's dream – not necessarily our own – we must get our own egos out of the way. And that is usually a hard lesson to learn, because we tend to try to achieve the dream in our own strength. The reality we must accept is that we may be able to achieve earthly goals (the natural), but we cannot do the supernatural. Sandra Kennedy puts it this way: "I can do many things, but I cannot do things which are of the *kingdom*. I cannot do kingdom work *until* I get myself out of the way."

There are many people doing great things and fulfilling their own earthly dreams. They might be doing this by following good and even biblical principles. But if we want to fulfil God's higher purposes and dreams for our lives, we need to come to the realization that *we* can't do it in our own strength.

We need to learn to give God room to accomplish what we cannot do. This usually takes a long time to understand and accept. "But here is the secret," Sandra Kennedy explains. "The more I get myself out of the way, the higher I go." All the leaders interviewed for this book came to that realization: that they could not accomplish their God-given dream or calling by themselves. They learned to surrender in humility and got themselves – their own striving – out of the way. Then God began to do incredible things through them.

It's important to note that understanding that we can't do something on our own should not be confused with insecurity or a low self-image. Instead, it involves trusting God and really believing that he can do what he has said he will do through us. In order for this to happen, we cannot look down on ourselves. We have to believe that Christ is in us as much as he is in any person. We tend to measure ourselves by "great" people, and we often think that their successes came because they had special favour or anointing, or at least certain privileges, advantages, or talents. However, it is not a person who is anointed – it is *Christ in a person.* The more we understand that the secret is *Christ in us,* and the more we get ourselves out of the way and give him room, the more his anointing can flow through us (see John 3:30).

Priority shift

When we die to ourselves, another important shift happens in our lives. We are no longer focused on chasing our dream, but on chasing the dream giver. At that point, the fulfilment of our dream becomes a secondary pursuit. Our primary goal changes to knowing Christ. And then when we do see God's promises and purposes fulfilled through our lives, we are certain that *he* made it happen, and we are thrilled that we were able to participate. We know that we didn't make anything happen by ourselves; instead, Christ did it in us and through us. The apostle Paul puts it this way: "Not that we are adequate in ourselves to consider anything as *coming* from ourselves, but our adequacy is from God" (2 Corinthians 3:5, NASB). The reward and adventure of pursuing a God-given dream is to see Christ working through us and fulfilling the dream *with* us. That usually goes beyond what we could ever ask, dream, or imagine! This in turn leads us into a more intimate relationship with Jesus and a deeper love for him. And that is the real point.

When Rolland Baker was trying to decide his direction in life, he felt too inadequate to follow in the footsteps of his parents and grandparents and become a missionary. He saw them as spiritual giants – especially his grandfather. "I felt I wasn't spiritual enough to be a missionary and do what my grandfather did, so I decided to do what I *could* do. I was good at science, so I thought it would be a good idea to become a scientist," he says.

But the night before he was to enrol at university, he realized that, twenty years down the road, it would be infinitely more important to him to know God as deeply as possible than to be a scientist and just know his creation. "It's all about how well we can get to know God in this life," Rolland points out. "There is only really one purpose for our soul in life and that's to get to know Jesus as well as we can. But we get so busy that we make the work or dream our sole purpose. But the real point is our love for God."

Rolland's experience doesn't mean everyone must become a missionary in order to get to know God as well as possible. This was the specific decision that he faced, because of his background and calling in life. It could have easily been the other way around. We each must engage in the journey God has called us to and, within that journey, get to know him.

Treasures of darkness

Does it always take suffering or a valley of testing to learn to chase the dream giver? Not always, but usually. Rolland Baker says he knows some people who have had incredible supernatural experiences: visions, miracles, amazing encounters with God. They seem to have reached their dream without experiencing much suffering in their lives. But he has also observed that these same people don't always react well when something does go seriously wrong. When difficult situations arise, they become uncertain and sometimes question God.

The point, however, is not the suffering itself. Suffering doesn't do anything except make us suffer. But when we allow God to work through the suffering to draw us closer to him, we can find treasures in the midst of darkness. The thing about treasures is that they are usually hidden, and darkness alone doesn't make them visible. But when we seek God in the times of darkness and let him work to transform us, he reveals the treasures that can only be found in those dark places: "I will give you the treasures of darkness and riches hidden in secret places, so that you may know that it is I, the Lord, the God of Israel, who call you by your name" (Isaiah 45:3, NRSVA).

When we face the difficulties in our lives *with* God, he can transform us.

Suffering for the sake of Jesus and the kingdom can build character and love in us. This is something that the persecuted church understands. As Andrew White says, the suffering Christians in Baghdad are the happiest people he knows. He remembers his church in Baghdad as the most joyful place on earth. How is that possible? Because the people have truly tapped into the glorious riches that are in Christ and come to understand that there is an inheritance that goes beyond the realization of our dreams on earth. Our inheritance is Christ himself and the riches hidden in him (see Hebrews 11:13).

Qualities of a godly leader

Desmond Tutu's views on the qualities of a good and godly leader can help us understand why some people's preparation processes on the way to their destiny are so demanding. "Ultimately, you want a leader who is also a servant. Leaders are leaders because they are servants. When you look at some of the greatest leaders in history you will see that they were not in it for their own aggrandizement."

Tutu shared more of his thoughts on leadership in his interview with Swedish journalist Marika Griehsel. "A good leader leads on behalf of and for the sake of the people, and, almost always, a great leader will show just how he or she is a leader for the sake of the people *by suffering*." Tutu explains that great leaders do not seek self-glorification, nor do they try to build their own nests – but many "wannabe" leaders do. He says, "You can look at leaders like Nelson Mandela, Mahatma

Gandhi, or Mother Teresa, and you will see that a common characteristic is that they were doing something sacrificial for the sake of those they were serving."[4] They accepted the high calling and learned to continually lay down their lives for the sake of those they were serving.

This is the leadership Jesus modelled, which is why he is often called the suffering servant. Godly leaders are there for the sake of those who are being led. They lay down their lives for their people. Thus, when God calls someone to a higher level of leadership, the training and preparation process is elaborate and difficult. If, as described in Hebrews 5:8, Jesus himself "learned obedience by the things which he suffered", we can expect the same. But we can also expect to share in the rewards. The Greek word for obedience in this passage means "to hear and listen attentively".[5] So we too can learn to hear and listen attentively through suffering. From listening, we gain insight into the Father's heart and what he wants to do, and then we can be his hands and feet and obey him.

Understanding your journey

Everyone's journey is unique, and everyone's calling, dream, and assignment on earth is different. But we know this: we were created for good works in Christ Jesus, which he has already prepared for us before the foundation of the world (Ephesians 2:10). Maybe you can't yet see the whole picture of the works prepared for you, or you might not yet have any idea of them at all. But we can be confident that as we pursue our relationship with Jesus, growing closer to him and working with him, he will lead us to discover them.

Perhaps he will have you impact the world or a whole nation. It may be that the works he has for you are in your family, in your community, at your workplace. Or it may be that he has called you solely to minister to him. But don't compare yourself or attempt to imitate others. It's important to find *your* place, because that will be the most fulfilling place for you. If William Paul Young had tried to do what Andrew White did he would have been miserable. If Desmond Tutu had tried to fulfil Bill Johnson's call he would have been ineffective. If Heidi Baker had tried to take Sandra Kennedy's place, or the other way around, they would have ended up frustrated. If you and I try to imitate the works of someone we look up to we will only find ourselves disillusioned and left with the feeling that we don't measure up.

So you have to find *your* place, and you can only find that by connecting with what God has put in your heart from before the foundation of the world. And he will reveal it as you pursue your relationship with him, learn to listen to him, and act on it.

You also need to understand the unique way God speaks to you. We can't measure ourselves by the experiences of Loren Cunningham, Sandra Kennedy, or Heidi Baker – people who have experienced clear visions and visitations from the Lord. God considered it necessary to speak in such a way, possibly because of the nature of their calling, or the direction they might have pursued for their lives otherwise.

Sandra Kennedy's experience illustrates another important truth: when God has called you and set you apart for a certain task, he will continue to move you in the right direction. Remember, it took three identical supernatural visions and more than eleven years before Sandra finally stepped into her calling. God doesn't simply move on and leave us behind when we miss the vision or struggle with our weaknesses and insecurities. God is faithful, and he is more interested in bringing us into the fullness of our destiny and calling than we are.

The only way we can sabotage this is when we willingly choose to walk away and refuse to cooperate with God. So often, when difficulties come our way, we think we have missed God's call; that at some point we have failed or forfeited our calling. But it's crucial to understand that, in those seasons, God is building within us character, perseverance, and the right focus – which is Christ. The works he has for us are secondary, flowing out of our relationship with him and our identity in him. If we try to find our identity in the works themselves, we will not see the fullness of what God can and wants to do through us.

Everybody has a story. In fact, everybody is a story. And God is writing all the different chapters. In some, he works in us; in others, he works through us. Wherever you are, whatever God has put in your heart and called you to, whatever your journey looks like right now, God has a dream, and that dream is that we live in unity with him and become all that we were created to be. He wants to fulfil his purposes on earth through us. All we have to do is share his desire, surrender to his transformation work in our hearts, and let the journey unfold!

Epilogue

Happily Ever After?

It was a beautiful late summer Tuesday morning when I was walking with my friends at the beach in Fish Hoek, South Africa. We were enjoying the sun and the magnificent view of False Bay at the Cape Peninsula while passing time before my interview with Floyd and Sally McClung that afternoon. I was excited to meet them and looking forward to drawing on the wealth of a lifetime of experience and wisdom as real pillars and pioneers in missions. Suddenly my phone rang. It was Floyd's assistant. "Floyd's asked me to call you to let you know that unfortunately he needs to postpone the interview. He's been rushed into hospital." She was going to get back to me later that week to reschedule once Floyd was out of hospital. That was 23 February 2016. Floyd has been in hospital ever since. That morning he woke up with severe, unbearable pain in his left leg and within hours he ended up in ICU. What started as a very rare virus infection led to sepsis and coma, leaving his life hanging by a thread and his left side paralyzed. The doctors didn't expect him to live more than four months.

God had been speaking to Floyd about 2016 being a year of breakthrough – and although Floyd's life was spared and both Sally and Floyd have had some breakthroughs in this roller-coaster ordeal, their faith and patience has been tested severely and the breakthrough of full restoration has not come yet. Despite prayers all around the world, Floyd is immobile to this day, unable to speak and dependent on full-time care in hospital. Sally was still recovering from ovarian cancer and both thought they had overcome the worst crisis of their lives, when suddenly Floyd's life was hanging by a thread. On top of that, Sally's cancer returned, she had multiple surgeries with complications and chemotherapy, which weakened her body so severely that they had to stop the procedure.

And yet, in all of this they are more than overcomers. They have become true faith heroes. I am moved beyond words when Sally shares in her updates that even though she cannot understand and is at the end of her strength, all she can do is keep trusting God's faithfulness. And that although Floyd is emotional and can only communicate with smiles or tears, he still raises his right arm (which has some mobility) in worship when she and the care team sing worship songs in the hospital room. Even though Floyd is unable to speak or sing, this testimony speaks louder than any spoken sermon. The depth of our faith does not show on the mountaintops but in the valley of the shadow of death when we are faced with unexplainable contradictions.

Why am I sharing this story? Do all stories end in a happily ever after? Not on this side of eternity. That's why it is so important to learn not to judge according to circumstances, but to keep looking to the reward that transcends our time on earth and understand that the manifestation of breakthrough is not the defining element for real success. Faithfulness is.

It is not time to sit back when we have experienced a breakthrough. Rolland Baker shares from his own experience: "We often turn to God in times of crisis, but once they are over, we tend to go on with our lives and ease off. But when you've lived through several of these cycles you know that times of blessing are not times to ease off, but to draw closer to God."

I started my series of interviews in 2013 and since my last interview in 2016, the lives of the interviewees have taken different turns and been hit by new challenges. I already mentioned in Chapter Two that the cancer Les Brown had been fighting returned and spread to four of his vertebrae in his back, causing extreme pain and demanding aggressive medication. The doctors told him to settle his affairs, but Les refused to bow to cancer and instead keeps holding his course. He continues to be a living example of faith and a voice of hope and is determined to pursue the fullness of his calling despite the circumstances. Do the circumstances discourage him at times? Yes, they do. But he knows that his time has not yet come and he says that he aspires to inspire until he expires! When life knocks him down, he keeps getting up again and fights to get the upper hand.

Rolland Baker faced setbacks in his recovery, and the battle for his health took eight years in total. Andrew White has experienced severe deterioration in his body caused by MS, and his wife Caroline was diagnosed with MS as well. In 2017 she was so ill that Andrew didn't know if she would survive – and he didn't know what to pray for: that God would take her or that he would heal her. God did intervene and she is in recovery, but they both need full-time carers now. Andrew says he has had to make adjustments in his work as he is now mostly confined to a wheelchair. But the circumstances do not deter him from doing what God has called him to do.

Bill Johnson's life was hanging by a thread in 2017 when the doctors could not find out why he couldn't eat or drink, and why his body would reject all food and liquids. But Bill kept his eyes on God's promises for his life and walked through this valley with quiet trust in him.

Loren Cunningham's wife Darlene was seriously ill in 2017 as they pursued the vision to abolish Bible poverty by reaching unreached people groups in the Pacific. Thankfully, she recovered, but as the vision grows, so do the challenges.

The question is not why difficulties happen. The question is how to deal with them. It's also not a question of whether they will happen – they inevitably will. The purpose of this book is to show how others who have gone before us have navigated difficult seasons in life, and I hope you can draw hope and wisdom from the life lessons of these leaders. However, in the end it all comes down to this: our only safeguard is our trust that God is good, no matter what the circumstances say and no matter how they turn out. Our relationship with God is our anchor in times of trouble.

May it be so for you.

Acknowledgments

I am deeply grateful for all the friends who have supported me in my endeavour. Without you I could never have completed this project. I consider my friends all over the world the greatest asset I have, and I cherish every one of you! Since so many people have been involved in and touched my life, I cannot mention everyone by name. I have to restrict myself in this section to those who have been of great support in these past years while I was pursuing the Dream Chasers project.

First of all, I want to thank all the leaders who have made themselves available for this project and given me their time. This includes all the assistants who have diligently forwarded my interview requests and correspondence! I'm particularly grateful to Les Brown for believing in me and in my vision, and for encouraging me to pursue all that God has placed in me. Your voice has made a huge difference in my life and interrupted the story of my internal dialogues, which sabotaged me for so long. Many thanks also to Andrew White for encouraging me and writing the foreword for this book.

I'm deeply grateful for my friends who have believed in this book and in what God was doing when I couldn't see it myself: Jim Dixon, Susan de Rouw, Melanie Renee Witten, Herman and Betsy Bouwhuizen, my Delft friends who gave me a roof over my head when I didn't have one: Birte, Vinnie, Leo and Wim, Djoeke and Martijn; and Tanya for an unforgettable South Africa trip. To my sisters, Coretta and Tamara: thanks for encouraging and supporting me in financially lean and emotionally tough times. So glad you are my sisters!

Thanks to Kyle Holland for words of wisdom and helping me believe in me. To David Aikman for good counsel concerning the publication. To Arwin Baauw for great coaching and input in developing the Dream Chasers mentorship program! To Andy Baker for being a "brother in crime" in planning an exit strategy and taking risks. To Stephanie Wetzel for great edits and pushing the book to a higher level of excellence. And last but not least, to the staff of Lion Hudson for believing in this book and taking it on!

To my friends in the US, in the Netherlands, in South Africa, and in Germany: I'm grateful for all of you!

References

Introduction

1   Larry Crabb, *Shattered Dreams. God's Unexpected Path to Joy*, Colorado Springs: WaterBrook, 2010, p. 5.

Prisoners of Destiny

1   Nelson Mandela, *Long Walk to Freedom*, Randburg: Macdonald Purnell, 1995, p. 229.

2   Spiros Zodhiates (ed.), *Hebrew-Greek Key Word Study Bible: Lexical Aids to the Old Testament*, Chattanooga: AMG Publishers, 1991, p. 1654.

3   Nelson Mandela, *Long Walk to Freedom*, p. 372.

4   Nelson Mandela, *Long Walk to Freedom*, p. 689.

Winning the Battle of the Mind

1   Caroline Leaf, *Who Switched off My Brain?*, Southlake: Thomas Nelson Publishers, 2009, p. 40.

2   Wallace D. Wattles (1910), *The Science of Getting Rich: The Original Classic*, Oxford: Capstone Publishing, 2010.

Camped at the Gates of Hell

1   Heidi Baker, *Compelled by Love: How to Change the World by the Simple Power of Love in Action*, Lake Mary, Florida: Charisma House, 2008, p. xi.

2   Heidi Baker, *Compelled by Love*, pp. 9–10.

Enduring Faith

1   Loren Cunningham and Janice Rogers, *Is That Really You, God? Hearing the Voice of God*, Seattle: YWAM Publishing, 1984, p. 22.

2   Loren Cunningham and Janice Rogers, *Is That Really You, God?* p. 42.

3   Loren Cunningham and Janice Rogers, *Is That Really You, God?* p. 65.

4   Loren Cunningham and Janice Rogers, *Making Jesus Lord: The Dynamic Power of Laying Down Your Rights* (ebook), 1981.

5   Paul Gericke, *Crucial Experiences in the Life of D. L. Moody*, Chicago: Insight Press, 1978.

6   YWAM is moving fast toward this goal by partnering with many mission organizations and the body of Christ worldwide in the global campaign called End Bible Poverty Now. For this task YWAM is raising up a million intercessors to pray this vision into reality. You can get involved in praying for this endeavour by signing up at www.endbiblepovertynow.com.

Faith Under Fire

1   Andrew White, *My Journey So Far*, Oxford: Lion Hudson, 2015, p. 139.

2   Andrew White, *My Journey So Far*, p. 139.

Wounded Healers

1   Desmond and Mpho Tutu, *The Book of Forgiving: The Fourfold Path for Healing Ourselves and Our World*, London: HarperCollins, 2014, p. 67.

2   *Kaffir* is the Afrikaans equivalent of "nigger", a racially offensive term for black people in South Africa during apartheid.

3   Desmond and Mpho Tutu, *The Book of Forgiving*, p. 68.

4   Desmond and Mpho Tutu, *The Book of Forgiving*, p. 69.

5   Desmond and Mpho Tutu, *The Book of Forgiving*. The whole story is documented in full detail on pages 67–70.

6   'Desmond Tutu Interview/Part 1/Skavlan'. Available at https://www.youtube.com/watch?v=fdCiXOt0QQM, published 26 September 2014 (accessed 26 June 2018).

7   'The Frost Interview – Desmond Tutu: Not going quietly'. Available at https://www.youtube.com/watch?v=r3yxFzs73Ss, published 17 November 2012 (accessed 18 June 2018).

8   Allister Sparks and Mpho Tutu, *Tutu: Authorized*, Auckland: HarperCollins, 2010, p. 24.

9   Steven D. Gish, *Desmond Tutu: A Biography*, London: Greenwood Press, 2004, p. 3.

10   Steven D. Gish, *Desmond Tutu*, p. 9.

11   Steven D. Gish, *Desmond Tutu*, p. 10.

12   Steven D. Gish, *Desmond Tutu*, p. 28.

13   Steven D. Gish, *Desmond Tutu*, p. 34.

14   'Apartheid, Perpetrators, Forgiveness: Desmond Tutu's views'. Available at https://www.youtube.com/watch?v=eRDBWoV_hA0, published 20 April 2008 (accessed 18 June 2018).

15   'Apartheid, Perpetrators, Forgiveness', 20 April 2008.

16   For more details, see 'Desmond Tutu Truth and Reconciliation'. Available at https://www.youtube.com/watch?v=g6tJQRxxGTM&t=3s, published 22 October 2009 (accessed 18 June 2018).

17   'Desmond Tutu Truth and Reconciliation', 22 October 2009.

18   'Forgiveness is the key'. Available at https://www.youtube.com/watch?v=LZsYSH4f9QQ, published 17 November 2007 (accessed 18 June 2018).

19   'Apartheid, Perpetrators, Forgiveness', 20 April 2008.

20   'The Frost Interview – Desmond Tutu: Not going quietly', 17 November 2012.

21   Desmond and Mpho Tutu, *The Book of Forgiving*, p. 2.

22   'Archbishop Desmond Tutu on Forgiveness'. Available at https://www.youtube.com/watch?v=raG6eIL-LM0, published 6 January 2008 (accessed 18 June 2018).

23   'Forgiveness is the key', 17 November 2007.

24   'Forgiveness is the key', 17 November 2007.

25   Desmond and Mpho Tutu, *The Book of Forgiving*, p. 4.

26   'Apartheid, Perpetrators, Forgiveness', 20 April 2008.

27   Desmond and Mpho Tutu, *The Book of Forgiving*, p. 37.

28   'Desmond Tutu Truth and Reconciliation', 22 October 2009.

29   'Apartheid, Perpetrators, Forgiveness', 20 April 2008.

30   'Apartheid, Perpetrators, Forgiveness', 20 April 2008.

31   'Apartheid, Perpetrators, Forgiveness', 20 April 2008.

32   'Desmond Tutu, Peacemaker: A conversation with Desmond Tutu & John Allen'. Available at https://www.youtube.com/watch?v=hOaSbGD7Was&t=1277s, published 26 March 2013 (accessed 18 June 2018).

Will **YOU** Become
A **Dream Chaser?**

Are you ready to venture into your own journey as a dream chaser and follow the example of those who have gone before us?

If this book has inspired you and you know deep inside that more is possible than what you are experiencing right now then your time hascome to step out of the ordinary!

I am training ordinary people to discover their unique pathway towards the ext raordinary and to make a difference in this world to the people they love and care about.

If you are ready to move forward and to take the next step into your journey towards your destiny I have a **special gift** for you. I will give you the first step in the Dream Chasers Approach absolutely for **FREE**!

I wrote a special **E-course** for you that will launch you into your next step on your unique journey in becoming a true dream chaser!

This is what you will get

- hands-on assignments to discover who you really are and what you are about
- clarity on your life-purpose
- insight into your own process of growth and becoming a dream chaser
- focus to pursue your next step
- surprise bonus (for a limited time only!) upon handing in the assignments and engaging in the process.

Will you become a true dream chaser to manifest your dreams and help others make their dreams come true as well?

Then go to

www.dreamchasersapproach.com/ecourse

and claim your free spot!